"THE drama of Blackfeet covers a period of fully two centuries. It is replete with action and conflict, with some comedy and much tragedy. In the early years of the eighteenth century the Blackfeet were an independent, stone-age people. For more than a century thereafter they were the dominant military power on the northwestern plains, feared by all neighboring tribes, the inveterate enemies of white trappers. Only seventy-five years ago the extermination of the buffalo, their basic resource, quickly reduced these bold, proud people to a condition of dire poverty, making them dependent upon government rations for their daily bread. For many of them it has been a long, hard road back toward economic independence under radically changed conditions of life."

— John C. Ewers
The Blackfeet

MY LIFE AS AN INDIAN

The fascinating adventures of one man's sojourn in a primitive world.

My Life as an Indian

J. W. SCHULTZ

Fawcett Columbine ● New York

MY LIFE AS AN INDIAN

Published by Fawcett Columbine Books, CBS Educational and Professional Publishing, a division of CBS Inc., by arrangement with the author's estate.

ISBN: 0-449-90057-6

Printed in the United States of America

First Fawcett Columbine printing: October 1981

10 9 8 7 6 5 4 3

Contents

Principal Characters

NÄT-AH'-KI—A Blackfoot Indian girl who becomes the wife of the author.

THE CROW WOMAN—An Arickaree captured long ago by the Crows and later taken from them by the Bloods.

MRS. BERRY—A Mandan woman, wife of an old-time Indian trader, mother of Berry and friend of the Crow Woman; learned in the ancient lore of her tribe.

THE AUTHOR—At the age of twenty goes west to Montana Territory in search of wild life and adventure, and finds both with the Piegan Blackfeet; he marries into the tribe and lives with them for many years; goes with them on the hunt and on the warpath; joins in their religious ceremonies; and as a squawman lives the Indian life.

BERRY—A mixed-blood Indian trader, born on the upper Missouri River; speaks half a dozen Indian languages, and is very much at home in Indian camps; an adept at all the tricks of the Indian trade.

SORREL HORSE—White man, trapper, and Indian trader; has an Indian family.

FATHER PRANDO—A Jesuit priest whose life is given to mission work among the Indians. The Blackfeet's friend, comforter, and helper during the terrible Famine Year.

RISING WOLF—Early Hudson Bay man, typical trapper, trader, and interpreter of the romantic days of the early fur-trading period.

HEAVY BREAST—A Blackfoot partisan and leader of war parties.

WOLVERINE—A Blackfoot, brother-in-law of Sorrel Horse, whom the author helped to steal his wife.

WEASEL TAIL and TALKS-WITH-THE-BUFFALO—Blackfeet, close friends and hunting and war companions of the author.

CHAPTER 1

Fort Benton

THE love of wild life and adventure was born in me, yet I must have inherited it from some remote ancestor, for all my near ones were staid, devout people. I hated the conventions of society; in my New England town from my earliest memory I was happy only when, on school vacations, I was out in the great forest to the north, far beyond the sound of church and school bell, and the whistling locomotives. But a day came when I could go where and when I chose and one warm April morning, after a long trip, I left St. Louis on a Missouri River steamboat, bound for the Far West. My first destination was Fort Benton, Missouri Territory, 2600 miles up the Big Muddy.

I had read and re-read Lewis and Clark's *Journal,* Catlin's *Eight Years, The Oregon Trail,* Fremont's expeditions; at last I was to see some of the land and the tribes of which they told.

After we entered the buffalo country there were many places which I passed with regret; I wanted to stop off and explore them. But the captain of the flat-bottomed boat would say: "Don't get impatient; you must keep on to Fort Benton; that's the place for you, for there you'll meet traders and trappers from all over the Northwest, men you can rely upon and travel with. Good God, boy, suppose I should set you ashore here? Why, in all likelihood you wouldn't keep your scalp two days. These breaks and groves shelter many a prowlin' war party. You don't see 'em, but they're here all the same."

I could not bring myself to believe that I, I who thought so much of the Indians, and wanted to live with them, could possibly receive any harm at their hands. But one day, somewhere between the Round Butte and the mouth of the Musselshell River, we came upon a ghastly sight. On a shelving, sandy slope of shore, by a still smouldering fire of which their half-burned skiff formed a part, lay the remains of three white men. They had been scalped and cut to pieces, their heads crushed, hands and feet severed and thrown promiscuously about. We stopped and buried them. I did not again ask to be set ashore.

Ours was the first boat to arrive at Fort Benton that spring. Long before we came in sight of the place the inhabitants had seen the smoke of our craft and made preparations to receive us. When we turned the bend and neared the levee, cannon boomed, flags waved, and the entire population assembled on the shore to greet us. Foremost in the throng were the two traders who had some time before bought out the American Fur Company, fort and all. They wore suits of blue broadcloth, their long-tailed, high-collared coats bright with brass buttons; they wore white shirts and stocks, and black cravats; their long hair, neatly combed, hung down to their shoulders. Beside them were their skilled employees—clerks, tailor, carpenter— and they wore suits of black fustian, also brass-buttoned, and their hair was likewise long, and they wore parfleche-soled moccasins, gay with intricate and flowery designs of cut beads. Behind these prominent personages the group was most picturesque; here were the French employees, mostly creoles from St. Louis and the lower Mississippi, men who had passed their lives in the employ of the American Fur Company, and had cordelled many a boat up the vast distances of the winding Missouri. These men wore the black fustian capotes, or hooded coats, fustian or buckskin trousers held in place by sashes. Then there were bull-whackers, and mule-skinners, and independent traders and trappers, most of them attired in suits of plain or fringed and beaded buckskin, and nearly all of them had knives and Colt's powder-and-ball six-shooters stuck in their belts; and their headgear, especially that of the traders

and trappers, was home-made, being generally the skin of a
kit fox roughly sewn in circular form, head in front and tail
hanging down behind. Back of the whites were a number of
Indians, men and youths from a near-by camp, and women
married to the resident and visiting whites. I had already
learned from what I had seen of the various tribes on our way
up the river that the ordinary Indian of the plains is not the
gorgeously attired, eagle-plume bedecked creature various
prints and written descriptions had led me to believe he was.
Of course, all of them possessed such fancy attire, but it was
worn only on state occasions. Those I now saw wore leather
leggings, plain or beaded moccasins, calico shirts, and either
blanket or leather toga. Most of them were bareheaded, their
hair neatly braided, and their faces were painted with reddish-
brown ochre or Chinese vermilion. Some carried a bow and
quiver of arrows; some had flintlock fukes, a few the more
modern caplock rifle. The women wore dresses of calico; a few
"wives" of the traders and clerks and skilled laborers even wore
silk, and gold chains and watches, and all had the inevitable
gorgeously hued and fringed shawl thrown over their shoulders.

At one glance the eye could take in the whole town, as it
was at that time. There was the great rectangular adobe fort,
with bastions mounting cannon at each corner. A short distance above it were a few cabins, built of logs or adobe. Back
of these, scattered out in the long, wide flat-bottom, lay camp
after camp of trader and trapper, string after string of canvas-
covered freighters' wagons, and down at the lower end of the
flat were several hundred lodges of Piegans. All this motley
crowd had been assembling for days and weeks, impatiently
awaiting the arrival of the steamboats. The supply of provisions
brought up by the boats the previous year had fallen far short
of the demand. There was no tobacco to be had at any price.
Keno Bill, who ran a saloon and gambling house, was the only
one who had any liquor, and that was alcohol diluted with
water, four to one. He sold it for a dollar a drink. There was
no flour, no sugar, no bacon in the town, but that did not

matter, for there was plenty of buffalo and antelope meat. What all craved, Indians and whites, was tobacco and liquor. And here it was, a whole steamboat load, together with groceries; no wonder cannon boomed and flags waved, and the population cheered when the boat hove in sight.

I went ashore and put up at the Overland Hotel, which was a fair-sized log cabin with a number of log-walled additions. For dinner we had boiled buffalo boss ribs, bacon and beans, biscuit, coffee with sugar, molasses, and stewed dried apples. The regular guests scarcely touched the meat, but the quantities of bread, syrup, and dried apples they stowed away was surprising.

I had letters of introduction to the firm which had bought out the American Fur Company. They received me kindly and one of them took me around introducing me to the various employees, residents of the town, and to several visiting traders and trappers. Of the latter I met a man only a few years older than myself, who I was told was the most successful and daring of all the traders of the plains. He spoke a number of Indian languages perfectly, and was at home in the camps of any of the surrounding tribes. The Indians called him the Berry.

It was not half an hour after the arrival of the steamboat, before whisky dropped to the normal price of two bits per drink, and tobacco to $2 per pound. The white men, with few exceptions, hied to the saloons to drink, smoke, and gamble. Some hurried to load their wagons with kegs and make for the Indian camp. The Indians had prime buffalo robes, and they wanted whisky. They got it. By the time night closed in, the single street was full of them charging up and down on their pinto ponies, singing, yelling, recklessly firing their guns, and vociferously calling, so I was told, for more liquor. There was a brisk trade that night at the rear doors of the saloons. An Indian would pass in a good head and tail buffalo robe and receive for it two and even three bottles of liquor. He might just as well have walked boldly in at the front door and traded for it over the bar, I thought, but I learned that there was a

United States marshal somewhere in the Territory, and that there was no telling when he would turn up.

We went up the street to a fair-sized adobe cabin. Berry and I arrived at the open doorway and looked in. "Hello, Berry; come in, old boy," and *"Bon soir, Monsieur Berri, bon soir; entrez! entrez!"* some of the dancers shouted; we went in and took seats on a bench against the wall. All the females in the place were Indians, and for that matter they were the only women at that time in all Montana, barring a few white hurdy-gurdy girls at the mines of Helena and Virginia City.

These Indian women, as I had remarked in the morning when I saw some of them on the levee, were comely, of good figure and height, and neatly dressed, even if they were corsetless and wore moccasins; far different indeed from the squat, broad, dark natives of the Eastern forests I had seen. And they had much pride and dignity; that one could see at a glance. And yet they were jolly, chattering and laughing like so many white women. That surprised me. I had read that Indians were a taciturn, a gloomy, silent people, seldom smiling, to say nothing of laughing and joking with freedom and abandon.

"This," Berry told me, "is a traders' and trappers' dance. The owner of the house is not at home, or I would introduce you to him. As to the others—" with a sweep of his hand—"they're too busy just now for any introduction. I can't introduce you to the women, for they do not speak English. However, you must dance with some of them."

"But, if they do not speak our language, how am I to ask them to dance?"

"Walk up to one you choose, and say 'Ki-tak-stai pes-ka'— will you dance?"

A quadrille had just ended. I boldly walked up to the nearest woman, repeating the words over and over that I might not forget them, bowed politely, and said, "Ki-tak-stai peska?"

The woman laughed, nodded, and replied, "Ah," which I later learned was yes, and extended her hand; I took it and led her to a place for another quadrille just forming. While we were waiting she spoke to me several times, but I could only shake my head and say: "I do not understand." She laughed and spoke in her language to her neighbor, another comely young woman, who also laughed and looked at me with amusement in her eyes. I began to feel embarrassed.

The music struck up and I found that my partner was a light and graceful dancer. I forgot my embarrassment and enjoyed the quadrille, my strange partner, the strange music, and strange surroundings immensely.

The quadrille ended; I started to lead my partner to a seat, but instead she led me over to Berry, who had also been dancing, and spoke rapidly to him for a moment.

"This," said he to me, "is Mrs. Sorrel Horse. She invites us to accompany her and her husband home and have a little feast."

Of course we accepted and after a few more dances departed. I had been introduced to Sorrel Horse. He was a very tall, slender man, sorrel-haired, sorrel-whiskered, blue-eyed; a man, as I afterward learned, of extremely happy temperament under the most adverse conditions, a sincere friend to those he liked, but a terror to those who attempted to wrong him.

Sorrel Horse's home was a fine large Indian lodge of eighteen skins, set up beside his two canvas-covered wagons near the river's bank. His wife built a little fire, made some tea, and presently set before us some Dutch oven baked biscuits, broiled buffalo tongue, and stewed bull berries. We heartily enjoyed the meal, and I was especially taken with the luxurious comfort of the lodge: the soft buffalo robe couch upon which we sat, the sloping willow back rests at each end of it, the cheerful little fire in the center, the oddly shaped, fringed and painted parfleches in which Madam Sorrel Horse kept her provisions and her various belongings. It was all new and delightful to me, and when after a smoke and a chat, Sorrel Horse said: "You had better camp here for the night, boys," my happiness was complete. We went to sleep on the couch covered with soft blankets and listening to the soft murmur of the river's current.

CHAPTER 2

The Girl-Hunt

IT was agreed that I should join Berry in the autumn, when he would begin the season's trade with the Indians. He owned a large bull-train, with which he hauled freight from Fort Benton to the mining camps in summer, finding in that more profit than in trading for the deer, elk, and antelope skins, which were about the only things of value that the Indians had to barter at that season. Buffalo robes were valuable only from animals killed from November to February inclusive. I wanted to hunt and travel in this land of glorious sunshine and dry, clear air; so I bought a roll of bedding, large quantities of tobacco, and .44 rimfire cartridges for my Henry rifle, a trained buffalo horse and saddle, and pulled out of the town with Sorrel Horse.

Sorrel Horse's wagons, a lead and a trail, drawn by an eight-horse team, were heavily loaded with provisions and trade goods, for he was going with a band of the Piegans, the Small Robes, on their summer hunt. And this was what had made me at once accept his invitation to accompany him. I would have an opportunity to study the people.

Sorrel Horse's brother-in-law, Lis'-sis-tsi, Wolverine, and I became great friends. I soon learned to use the sign language, and he helped me in my studies of the Blackfoot language.

Part of that summer we passed at the foot of the Belt Mountains, and part on Warm Spring Creek and the Judith River. I joined in the buffalo runs, and on my swift and well-trained horse managed to kill my share of the animals. I hunted antelope, elk, deer, bighorn, and bear with Wolverine.

There were days when Wolverine went about with a long face and a preoccupied air, never speaking except to answer some question. One day in August when he was in this mood I asked what was troubling him.

"There is nothing troubling me," he replied. Then after a long silence; "I lied; I am in great trouble. I love Piks-ah'-ki and she loves me, but I cannot have her; her father will not give her to me. Her father is a Gros Ventre, but her mother is Piegan. Long ago my people protected the Gros Ventres, fought their battles, helped them to hold their country against all enemies. And then the two tribes quarreled, and for many years were at war with each other. This last winter they made peace. It was then I first saw Piks-ah'-ki. She is very beautiful; tall, long hair, eyes like an antelope, small hands and feet. I went much to her father's lodge, and we would look at each other when the others there were not noticing. One night I was standing by the doorway of the lodge when she came out for an armful of wood from the big pile lying there. I took hold of her and kissed her, and she put her arms around my neck and kissed me back. That is how I know she loves me. Do you think that she would have done that if she did not love me?"

"No, I do not think she would."

His face brightened and he continued: "At that time I had only twelve horses, but I sent them to her father with a message that I would marry his daughter. He sent the horses back and these words: 'My daughter shall not marry a poor man!'

"I went with a war party against the Crows and drove home eight head of their best horses. I traded for others until I had thirty-two in all. I sent a friend with them to the Gros Ventre camp to ask once more for this girl; he returned, driving back the horses. This is what her father said: 'My daughter shall never marry Wolverine, for the Piegans killed my son and my brother.'" He looked at me hesitatingly two or three times and finally said: "The Gros Ventres are encamped on the Missouri, at the mouth of this little (Judith) river. I am going to steal the girl from her people; will you go with me?"

"Yes," I quickly replied. "I'll go with you, but why don't you ask some of the Raven Carriers to go with you, as you belong to that society?"

"Because," he replied, "because I might fail to get the girl; she might even refuse to go with me, and then my good friends would tell about it, and people would jeer at me. But if I fail I know you will never tell about it."

One evening about dusk we quietly left the camp. No one except Sorrel Horse knew of our departure. But genial old Sorrel Horse laughed when I told him where we were going.

We left the camp at dusk, for it was not safe to ride over the plains in the daytime; too many war parties of various tribes were abroad, seeking glory and wealth in the scalps and chattels of unwary travelers. We rode out of the Judith valley eastward on to the plain, and when we were far enough out to avoid the deep coulées running into it, turned and paralleled the course of the river. Wolverine led a lively but gentle pony on which we had packed some bedding and a large bundle done up in a fine buffalo robe and bound with many a thong. These things he had taken out of camp the night before and hidden in the brush. There was a glorious full moon, and we were able to trot and lope along at a good pace. We had not traveled many miles from camp before we began to hear the bellowing of the buffalo; it was their mating season and the bulls kept up a continuous deep, monotoned bellow as they charged and fought from band to band of the great herds. Several times during the night we rode close to a band and startled them, and they ran off thundering over the hard ground and rattling their hoofs, away in the soft moonlight; we could hear them still running long after they had disappeared from view. It seemed as if all the wolves in the country were abroad that night, for they could be heard in all directions, near and far, mournfully howling.

On Wolverine went, urging his horse and never looking

back, and I kept close and said nothing, although I thought the pace too fast. When at last day began to break we found ourselves in a country of high pine-clad buttes and ridges, and two or three miles from the Judith valley. Wolverine stopped and looked around.

"So far as I can see," he said, "everything looks well. The buffalo and antelope feed quietly. But even now some enemy may be sitting in the pines of those buttes looking down upon us. Let us hurry to the river—we must have water—and hide in the timber in the valley."

We unsaddled in a grove of cottonwoods and willows and led our horses to water. On a wet sand bar where we came to the stream there were a number of human footprints so recently made that they seemed to be as fresh as our own tracks. The sight startled us and we looked about anxiously, holding our rifles ready. There was no timber on the opposite side of the stream at that point, and we had just come through the grove above us, so we realized that the makers of the tracks were not in our immediate vicinity.

"Crees, or men from across the mountains," said Wolverine, again examining the tracks. "No matter which; they are all our enemies."

We drank our fill and went back into the grove, tying our horses so that they could graze.

"How could you know," I asked, "that those whose tracks we saw are not Crows, or Sioux, or other people of the plains?"

"The footprints were wide, rounding; even the prints of their toes could be seen; because they wore soft-bottom moccasins. Only those people use such footwear; all those of the plains here wear moccasins with hard parfleche soles.

"I will go around the inner edge of the grove and have a look at the country."

Presently Wolverine returned. "The war party passed through the grove," he said, "and went on down the valley. About two nights from now they will be trying to steal the Gros Ventre horses. Well, we will eat."

He undid the buffalo robe bundle and spread out a number of articles; heavy red and blue cloth, enough for two dresses. The stuff was made in England and the traders sold it for about $10 a yard. Then there were strings of beads, brass rings, silk handkerchiefs, Chinese vermilion, needles, thread, earrings— an assortment of things dear to the Indian women.

"For her," he said, laying them carefully aside.

That was a long day. By turns we rested; I scarcely dozed, for I was always expecting the war party to jump us. Yes, I was pretty young at the business then, and so was the Indian. What we ought to have done, after getting water, was to have ridden to the top of some butte and remained there during the day. From such a point we could have seen the approach of an enemy a long way off, and our horses could easily have taken us beyond his reach. It was mere luck that we were not seen to enter the valley and the cottonwood grove, for there a war party could have surrounded us and rendered our escape impossible.

Up to this time Wolverine had made no definite plan to get the girl away. Sometimes he would say that he would steal into the camp and to her lodge at night, but that was certainly risky, for if he did succeed in getting to the lodge without being taken for an enemy come to steal horses he might awaken the wrong woman and then there would be a terrible outcry. On the other hand, if he boldly went into the camp on a friendly visit, no doubt old Bull's Head, the girl's father, would suspect his purpose and closely watch her. But this discovery of a war party moving down the river toward the Gros Ventre camp gave him a plain opening.

"I knew that my medicine would not desert me," he suddenly said that afternoon. "We will ride boldly into camp, to the lodge of the great chief, Three Bears. I will say that our chief sent me to warn him of a war party working this way. I will say that we ourselves have seen their tracks along the bars of the river. Then the Gros Ventres will guard their horses; they will ambush the enemy; there will be a big fight, big excitement.

All the men will rush to the fight, and that will be my time.
I will call Piks-ah'-ki, we will ride out fast."

Again we rode hard all night, and at daylight came in sight
of the wide dark gash in the great plain which marked the
course of the Missouri. We had crossed the Judith the evening
before, and were now on a broad trail worn in deep furrows by
the travois and lodge poles of many a camp of Piegans and Gros
Ventres, traveling between the great river and the mountains
to the south. The sun was not high when at last we came to
the pine-clad rim of the valley and looked down into the wide,
long bottom at the mouth of the Judith; there, gleaming against
the dark foliage of a cottonwood grove, were the lodges of the
Gros Ventres. Hundres of horses were feeding on the sage brush
flat; riders were galloping here and there, driving their bands
to water, or catching up fresh animals for the daily hunt. Although still a couple of miles away we could hear the confused
noise of the camps, shouts, childish laughter, singing, the beating of drums.

We rode into the camp stared at by all as we passed along.
The chief's lodge was pointed out to us. We dismounted at the
doorway, a youth took charge of our horses and we entered.
Three or four guests were enjoying an early feast and smoke.
The chief, Big Belly, motioned us to the seat of honor on his
own couch at the back of the lodge. He was a heavy, corpulent
man, a typical Gros Ventre.

The pipe was passed and we smoked a few whiffs from it in
our turn. A guest was telling a story, when he finished it the
chief turned to us, and asked, in good Blackfoot, whence we
had come. Nearly all the older Gros Ventres spoke Blackfoot
fluently, but the Blackfoot never could speak Gros Ventre; it
was too difficult for anyone not born and reared with them to
learn.

"We come," Wolverine replied, "from up the Yellow (Judith)
river, above the mouth of the Warm Spring. My chief, the Big
Lake, gives you this—" producing and handing him a long coil
of rope tobacco—"and asks you to smoke with him in friendship."

"Ah!" said Three Bears, smiling, and laying the tobacco to one side. "Big Lake is my good friend."

"My chief also sends word with me that you are to keep close watch of your horses, for some of our hunters have found signs of a war party traveling this way. We ourselves, this white man and I, we also have come across their trail. We saw it yesterday morning up the river. There are twenty, maybe thirty of them, and they are on foot. Perhaps tonight, surely by tomorrow night, they will raid your herd."

After our breakfast and another smoke, during which the chief asked questions about the Piegans, Wolverine and I strolled through the camp and down to the banks of the river. On the way he pointed out the lodge of his prospective father-in-law. Old Bull's Head was a medicine man, and the outside of his abode was painted with the symbols of his particular dream-given power, two huge grizzly bears in black, below which were circles of moons in red. We sat by the river a while, watching a lot of boys and young men swim; I noticed, however, that my companion kept an eye on the women continually coming for water. Evidently the particular one he longed to see did not appear, and finally we turned back toward the chief's lodge.

It was thought that the expected enemy would possibly arrive that night; so as soon as it was dark nearly all the men of the camp picked up their weapons and crept out through the sage brush to the foot of the hills, stringing out far above and below and back of their feeding herds. Wolverine and I had our horses up and saddled, and he told the chief that in case a fight began we would ride out and join his men. My comrade went out early in the evening, I sat up for an hour or more, and as he did not return, I lay down on the couch, covered myself with a blanket and was soon sound asleep, not waking until morning.

Wolverine was just getting up. After breakfast he told me that he had found a chance to whisper to Piks-ah′-ki the night before, when she had come outside for wood, and that she had agreed to go with him whenever the time came. He was in great spirits, and as we strolled along the shore of the river could not help breaking out in the war songs which the Blackfeet always sing when they are happy.

Along near noon, after we had returned to the lodge, among other visitors a tall, heavy, evil-featured man came in; by the nudge Wolverine gave me as he sat down opposite and scowled at us I knew that he was Bull's Head. He had a heavy growth of hair which he wore coiled on his head like a pyramid. He talked for some time with Three Bears and the other guests, and then, to my surprise, began to address them in Blackfoot, talking at us, and there was real and undisguised hatred in his tone.

"This story of an approaching war party," he said, "is all a lie. The Big Lake sends word that his people have seen their trail; now, I know that the Piegans are cowards; still, where there are so many of them they would be sure to follow such a trail and attack the enemy. No, they never saw any such trail, never sent any such word; but I believe an enemy has come, and is in our camp now, not after our herds but our women. Last night I was a fool. I went out and watched for horse stealers; I watched all night, but none came. Tonight I shall stay in my lodge and watch for women stealers, and my gun will be loaded. I advise you all to do the same."

And having had his say, he got up and strode out of the lodge, muttering, undoubtedly cursing all the Piegans, and one in particular. Old Three Bears watched him depart with a grim smile, and said to Wolverine:

"Do not remember his words; he is old, and cannot forget that your people killed his son and his brother. Others of us also lost brothers and sons in the war with your people, yet we made the great peace. The dead cannot be brought to life, but the living will live longer and be happier now that we have ceased to fight and rob one another."

"You speak the truth," said Wolverine. "Peace between us is good. I forget the old man's words. Guard your horses, for this night surely the enemy will come."

Again at dusk we saddled our horses and picketed them

close to the lodge. Wolverine put his saddle on the pinto pony and shortened the stirrups. He intended to ride his own animal bareback. He told me that Piks-ah'-ki had been under guard of her father's Gros Ventre wives all day; the old man not trusting her Piegan mother to accompany her after wood and water for the lodge. I again went to sleep early, my companion going out as usual.

This time I was awakened by the firing of guns out on the flat, and a great commotion in camp, men shouting and running toward the scene of the fight, women calling and talking excitedly, children shrieking. I hurried out to where our horses were picketed, carrying my own rifle and Wolverine's. I learned afterward that old Bull's Head was one of the first to rush to the rescue of his horses when the firing began. As soon as he had left the lodge Wolverine, who was lying nearby in the sage brush, ran to it and called his sweetheart's name. Out she came, followed by her mother, carrying several little bags. A minute later they came to where I stood, both women crying. Wolverine and I unfastened the horses.

"Hurry," he cried, "hurry."

He gently took the girl from where she was crying in the embrace of her mother and lifted her into the saddle, handing her the bridle reins.

"Listen," said the mother, "you will be good to her; I call the Sun to treat you as you do her."

"I love her, and I will be good to her," Wolverine answered, and then to us: "Follow me, hurry."

Away we went over the flat, straight for the trail upon which we had entered the valley, and straight toward the fight raging at the foot of the hill. We could hear the shots and shouts; see the flash of the guns. This was more than I had bargained for; I was sorry I had started out on this girl-stealing trip; I didn't want to charge in where the bullets of a fight that didn't interest me were flying. But Wolverine was leading, his sweetheart riding close behind him, and there was nothing for me to do but follow them. As we neared the scene my comrade began to shout:

"Where is the enemy? Kill all the horse thieves. Where are they? Where do they hide?"

I saw his point. He didn't intend that the Gros Ventres should mistake us for some of the raiders.

The firing had ceased and the shouting; but we knew that there in the moonlit sage brush both parties were lying, the one trying to sneak away, the other trying, without too much risk, to get sight of them. We had put a hundred yards or more now between us and the foot of the hill, and I was thinking that we were past the danger point when, with a sputter of fire from the pan and a burst of flame from the muzzle, a flint-lock gun crashed right in front of Wolverine. Down went his horse and he with it. Our own animals suddenly stopped. The girl cried out:

"They have killed him! Help, white man, they have killed him!"

But before we could dismount we saw Wolverine extricate himself from the fallen animal, spring to his feet and shoot at something concealed in the sage brush. We heard a deep groan, a rustling, and then Wolverine bounded to the place and struck something three or four hard blows with the barrel of his rifle. Stooping over, he picked up the gun which had been fired at him.

"I count a coup," he laughed, and running over to me and fastening the old fuke in the gun sling on the horn of my saddle, said, "Carry it until we get out of the valley."

I was about to tell him that I thought he was foolish to delay us for an old fuke, when right beside of us, old Bull's Head appeared, seeming to have sprung all at once out of the brush, and with a torrent of angry words he grasped the girl's horse by the bridle and attempted to drag her from the saddle. She shrieked and held on firmly, and then Wolverine sprang upon the old man, hurled him to the ground, wrenched his gun from him, and flung it far; then he leaped lightly up behind Piks-ah'-ki, dug his heels into the pony's flanks, and we were off once more, the irate father running after us and shouting for assistance to stop the runaways. We saw other Gros Ventres approaching, but they did not seem to be hurrying, nor did they attempt in any way to stop us. We went on as fast as we could up the steep, long hill.

We were four nights getting back to the Piegan camp, Wolverine riding part of the time behind me and part of the time behind the girl. We picked up, en route, the precious bundle which Wolverine had cached, and it was good to see the girl's delight when she opened it and saw what it contained. That day while we rested she made herself a dress from the red cloth, and I can truthfully say that when she had arrayed herself in it, and put on her beads and rings and earrings, she certainly looked fine. She was, as I afterward learned, as good as she was handsome. She made Wolverine a faithful and loving wife.

Fearing that we would be followed we had taken a circuitous route homeward, and made as blind a trail as possible, and upon our arrival at camp learned that old Bull's Head had got in there two days ahead of us. He was very different now from the haughty and malevolent man he had been at home. He fairly cringed before Wolverine, descanted upon his daughter's beauty and virtues, and said that he was very poor. Wolverine gave him ten horses and the fuke he had taken from the Indian he killed the night of our flight from the Gros Ventre camp. Old Bull's Head informed us that the war party were Crees, and that his people had killed seven of them, and that they had not succeeded in stealing a single horse, so completely were they surprised.

CHAPTER 3

The Fort on the Marias

ACCORDING to arrangement, I joined Berry at the end of August, and prepared to accompany him on his winter's trading expedition. He offered me a share in the venture, but I was not yet ready to accept it; I wanted to be absolutely free and independent for a few months more to go and come as I chose, to hunt, to roam about with the Indians and study their ways.

We left Fort Benton early in September with the bull train, creeping slowly up the hill out of the bottom, and scarcely any faster over the level of the now brown and dry plains. Bulls are slow travelers, and these had a heavy load to haul. The quantity and weight of merchandise that could be stowed away in those old-time prairie schooners were astonishing. Berry's train now consisted of four eight-yoke teams, drawing twelve wagons in all, loaded with fifty thousand pounds of provisions, alcohol, whisky, and trade goods. There were four bull-whackers, a night-herder who drove the "cavayard"—extra bulls and some saddle horses—a cook, three men who were to build the cabins and help with the trade, with Berry and his wife, and I. Not a very strong party to venture out on the plains in those times, but we were well armed, and hitched to one of the trail wagons was a six-pound cannon, the mere sight of which was calculated to strike terror to any hostiles.

Our destination was a point on the Marias River, some forty-five miles north of Fort Benton. Between that stream and the

Missouri, and north of the Marias to the Sweetgrass Hills and beyond, the country was dark with buffalo. Moreover, the Marias was a favorite stream with the Blackfeet for their winter encampments, for its wide, shallow valley was well timbered. In the shelter of the cottonwood groves their lodges were protected from the occasional north blizzards, there was an ample supply of fuel and fine grass for the horses. There were also great numbers of deer, elk, and mountain sheep in the valley and its breaks, and the skins of these animals were in constant demand; buckskin was largely used for the summer clothing and the footwear of the people.

September was the most perfect month of all the year in that region. To the west were the dark Rockies, their sharp peaks standing out sharply against the pale blue sky; northward were the three buttes of the Sweetgrass Hills; eastward dimly loomed the Bear Paws; south, away across the Missouri, the pine-clad Highwood Mountains were in plain sight; and between all these, around, beyond them, was the brown and silent plain, dotted with peculiar flat-topped buttes, deeply seamed with stream valleys and their numerous coulées.

We were nearly three days traveling the forty five miles to our destination. On all sides the buffalo and antelope grazed quietly, and those in our path did not run far to one side before they stopped, and began to crop the short grasses. We encamped the second night by a spring at the foot of the Goose Bill, a peculiarly shaped butte not far from the Marias. The wagons were drawn up in the form of a corral, as usual, and in the center of it our lodge was put up, a fine new one of sixteen skins. Berry and his wife, a couple of the men and I slept in it, the others making their beds in the wagons. We had a good supper, cooked over a fire of buffalo chips, and retired early.

Some time after midnight we were awakened by a heavy tramping in the corral; something crashed against a wagon on one side of us, and then against another on the other side. The men in the wagons began to call out, asking one another what was up; Berry told us to take our rifles and pile out. But before we could get out of bed something struck our lodge and over it went, the poles snapping and breaking, the lodge skin going on and careering about the corral as if it were endowed with life.

Mrs. Berry shrieked; men shouted to one another, and with one accord we all fled to the shelter of the wagons and hurriedly crept under them. Some one fired a shot at the gyrating lodge skin; Berry, who was beside me, followed suit, and then we all began to shoot, rifles cracking on all sides of the corral. For a minute, perhaps, the lodge skin whirled about, and dashed from one end of the corral to the other more madly than ever; and then it stopped and settled down upon the ground in a shapeless heap; from under it we heard several deep, rasping gasps, and then all was still.

Berry and I crawled out, walked cautiously over to the dim, white heap and struck a match. There we saw the body of a huge buffalo bull, still enveloped in the now tattered and ripped lodge covering. We could never understand how and why the old fellow wandered into the corral, nor why, when he charged the lodge, some of us were not trampled upon. Berry and his wife occupied the back side of the lodge, and he went right over them in his mad plunge, without putting a hoof on their bed.

We arrived at the Marias about noon the next day, and went into camp on a finely timbered point. After dinner the men began to cut logs for the cabins, and Berry and I rode up the river to hunt.

On our way up the river we saw many doe and fawn deer, a bunch of cow and calf elk, but not a buck or bull of either species. On our way homeward, however, along toward sunset, the male deer were coming in from the breaks and coulées to water, and we got a large, fat, buck mule deer. Madame Berry hung a whole forequarter of it over the lodge fire, and there it turned and slowly roasted for hours; about eleven o'clock she pronounced it done, and although we had eaten heartily at dusk, we could not resist cutting into it, and it was so good that in a short time nothing was left of the feast but the bones. I know of no way of roasting meat equal to this. You must have a lodge—to prevent draughts—a small fire; suspend the roast from a tripod above the blaze, and as it cooks give it an occasional twirl; hours are required to thoroughly roast it, but the result more than repays the labor involved.

The men soon cut and dragged out the required logs, put up the walls of our "fort," and laid on the roof of poles, which was covered with a thick layer of earth. When finished, it formed three sides of a square and contained eight rooms, each about sixteen feet square. There was a trade room, two living rooms, each of which had a rude but serviceable fireplace and chimney, built of mud-mortared stones. The other rooms were for storing merchandise and furs and robes. In the partitions of the trade room were numerous small holes, through which rifles could be thrust; at the back end of the square stood the six-pounder. With all these precautions for defense and offense, even the most reckless party of braves would think twice before making an attack upon the traders. But, of course, liquor was to be the staple article of trade, and no one could ever foretell what a crowd of drink-crazed Indians would do.

The fort was barely completed when the Piegan Blackfeet arrived, some 3500 of them, and pitched their lodges in a long, wide bottom about a mile below us. I passed the greater part of my time down in their camp with a young married man named Weasel Tail, and another who bore a singular name of Talks-with-the-buffalo. These two were inseparable companions, and they took a great liking to me, and I to them. Each had a fine new lodge, and a pretty young wife. I said to them once: "Since you think so much of each other, why not live together in one lodge? It would save much packing, much wear of horses when traveling, much labor setting up and breaking camp."

Talks-with-the-buffalo laughed heartily. "It is easy to see," he replied, "that you have never been married. Know this, my good friend: Two men will live together in quiet and lasting friendship, but two women never; they will be quarreling about nothing in less than three nights, and will try to drag their husbands into the row. That is the reason we live separately; to be at peace with our wives. As it is, they love each other, as my friend here and I love each other, and thus, for the good of us all, we have two lodges, two fires, two pack outfits, and enduring peace."

In that great camp of seven hundred lodges, I learned to gamble with the wheel and arrows, and with the bit of bone concealed in one or the other of the player's hands, and I even mastered the gambling song, which is sung when the latter game is being played around the evening lodge fire. Also, I attended the dances, and even participated in the one that was called "As-sin-ah-pes-ka"—Assiniboin dance.

In this Assiniboin dance, only young unmarried men and women participate. Their elders beat the drums and sing the dance song, which is a lively one, and of rather an abandoned nature. The women sit on one side of the lodge, the men on the other. The song begins, every one joining in. The dancers arise, facing each other, rising on their tip toes, and then sinking so as to bend the knees. Thus they advance and meet, then retreat, again advance and retreat a number of times, all singing, all smiling and looking coquettishly into each others' eyes. Thus the dance continues, perhaps for several hours, with frequent pauses for rest, or maybe to feast and smoke. But the fun comes in toward the close of the festivities; the lines of men and women have advanced; suddenly a girl raises her robe, casts it over her own and the head of the youth of her choice, and gives him a hearty kiss. The spectators shout with laughter, the drums are beaten louder than ever, the song increases in intensity. The lines retreat, the favored youth looking embarrassed, and all take their seats. For this kiss payment must be made on the morrow. If the young man thinks a great deal of the girl, he may present her with one or two horses; he must give her something, if only a copper bracelet or string of beads. I believe that I was an easy mark for those lively maidens, for I was captured and kissed more often than anyone else. And the next morning there would be three or four of them at the trading post with their mothers; and one must have numerous yards of bright prints; another some red trade cloth and beads; still another a blanket. They broke me, but still I would join in when another dance was given.

I spent hours and hours with the medicine men and old warriors, learning their beliefs and traditions, listening to their stories of the gods, their tales of war and the hunt. Also I attended the various religious ceremonies; listened to the appeals of the medicine men to the Sun as they prayed for health, long life, and happiness for the people. I learned much.

CHAPTER 4

A War Trip for Horses

THE young and middle-aged men of the tribes were constantly setting out for, or returning from war, in parties of from a dozen to fifty or more. That was their recreation, to raid the surrounding tribes who preyed upon their vast hunting ground, drive off their horses, and take scalps if they could. A few miles back from camp the returning warriors would don their picturesque war clothes, paint their faces, decorate their horses with eagle plumes and paint, and then ride quietly to the brow of the hill overlooking the village. There they would begin the war song, whip their horses into a mad run, and, firing guns and driving before them the animals they had taken, charge swiftly down the hill into the bottom. Long before they arrived the camp would be in an uproar of excitement, and the women, dropping whatever work they had in hand, would rush to meet them, followed more slowly and sedately by the men. How the women would embrace and hang on to their loved ones safely returned; and presently they could be heard chanting the praises of husband, or son, or brother.

No sooner did one of these parties return than others, incited by their success and anxious to emulate it, would form a party and start out against the Crows, or the Assiniboins, perhaps the Crees, or some of the tribes on the far side of the Backbone-of-the-world, as the Rockies were called. Therefore I was not surprised one morning to be told that they were about to start on a raid against the Assiniboins. "And you can go with us if you wish to," Talk-with-the-buffalo concluded. "You helped your friend to steal a girl, and you might as well try your hand at stealing horses."

"I will," I replied.

When I told Berry of my intention, both he and his wife protested strongly against it.

But my mind was made up; I was determined to go. There were to be thirty of us, and Heavy Breast, a grim and experienced warrior, was to be our partisan, or leader. He himself was the owner of a medicine pipe, which was considered to have great power. He had carried it on many an expedition, and it had always brought him and his parties good luck; taken them through various conflicts unharmed. But for all this, we had to get an old medicine man to pray with us in the sacred sweat lodge before we started, and to pray for us daily during our absence. Old Lone Elk was chosen for this responsible position; his medicine was of great power and had found favor with the Sun these many years. At the entrance of the sweat lodge we dropped our robes or blankets, our only covering, and creeping in at the low doorway, sat around the interior in silence while the red-hot stones were passed in and dropped in a hole in the center. Lone Elk began to sprinkle them with a buffalo tail dipped in water and as the stifling hot steam enveloped us he started a song of supplication to the Sun, in which all joined. Then the medicine pipe was filled, lighted with a coal which was passed in, and as it was passed around, each one, after blowing a whiff of smoke toward the heavens and the earth, made a short prayer to the Sun, to Old Man and Mother Earth. And when my turn came, I also made the prayer, audibly like the rest, and to the best of my ability.

It was getting late in the season, and the Assiniboins were thought to be a long way from us, somewhere near the mouth of the Little River, as the Blackfeet name the stream we call Milk River. It was decided that we should set out on horseback instead of afoot. The latter was the favorite way of making a raid, for a party traveling in that manner left no trail, and could conceal themselves during the daytime.

So one evening, led by our partisan, we rode southeastward over the dark plain, paralleling the river. My companions wore their plain, every-day leggings and shirt and moccasins and either the blanket or the cowskin toga. But tied to their saddles were their beautiful war clothes, and in a small parfleche cylinder their eagle plume or horn and weasel-skin headdresses. When going into battle, if there was time, these would be donned; if not, they would be carried into the fray, for they were considered to be great medicine, the shirt especially, upon which was painted its owner's dream, some animal or star or bird, which had appeared to him during the long fast he made before he changed from careless youth to responsible warrior.

After leaving the Marias, we were careful to conceal ourselves and our horses as well as possible during the daytime. We skirted the eastern slope of the Bear's Paw Mountains, the eastern edge of the Little Rockies—in Blackfoot, Wolf Mountains. Wherever we camped, sentinels were kept posted in a position overlooking the plains and mountains, and every evening they would report that the game was quiet, and that there was no sign of any persons except ourselves in all that vast region.

One morning at daylight we found ourselves at the foot of a very high butte just east of the Little Rockies, which I was told was the Hairy Cap, and well was it named for its entire upper portion was covered with a dense growth of pine. We went into camp at the foot of it, close to a spring and in a fine grassy glade entirely surrounded by brush. Talks-with-the-buffalo and I were told to ascend to the summit of the butte and remain there until the middle of the day, when others would take our place. We had both saved a large piece of roast buffalo ribs from the meal of the previous evening, so, drinking all the water we could hold and lugging our roast, we climbed upward on a broad game trail running through the pines, and finally reached the summit.

We found several war houses here, lodges made of poles, brush, pieces of rotten logs, so closely laid that not a glimmer

of a fire could shine through them. It was the way war parties
of all tribes had of building a fire for cooking or to warm themselves without betraying their presence to any passing enemy.
My companion pointed out one which he had helped build two
summers before, and he said that the butte was frequented by
war parties from all the tribes of the plains, because it commanded such an extended view of the country.

We sat down and ate our roast meat, and then Talks-with-
the-buffalo filled and lighted his black stone pipe and we
smoked. After a little I became very drowsy. "You sleep," said
Talks-with-the-buffalo, "and I will keep watch."

It was about ten o'clock when he awoke me. "Look! Look!"
he cried excitedly, pointing toward the Missouri. "A war party
coming this way."

Rubbing my eyes, I gazed in the direction indicated, and saw
bands of buffalo scurrying to the east, the west, and northward
toward us, and then I saw a compact herd of horses coming
swiftly toward the butte, driven by a number of riders. "They
are either Crees or Assiniboins," said my companion; "they
have raided the Crows or the Gros Ventres, and, fearing pursuit, are hurrying home."

We sped down the side of the butte. When we gave our news,
there was a rush to saddle horses, don war clothes and headdresses, and strip off shield coverings. And now Heavy Breast
himself ascended the side of the butte until he could get a view
of the oncoming party, while we waited for him at its base. He
stood there, perhaps a hundred yards from us, looking out over
the plain, and I thought that he never would come down and
give us his plan.

After a wait of five or ten minutes, Heavy Breast joined us.
"They will pass some distance east of here," he said. "We will
ride down this coulée and meet them." Every little way our
leader cautiously rode up to the edge of it and looked southward, and finally he called a halt. "We are now right in their
path," he said. "As soon as we can hear the beat of their horses'
hoofs we will dash up out of here at them."

My throat felt dry; I was scared. Like one in a daze, I heard

Heavy Breast give the command, and up we went out of the coulée, our leader shouting, "Take courage! Let us wipe them out!"

The enemy and the herd they were driving were not more than a hundred yards distant when we got upon a level with them, and our appearance was so sudden that their horses were stampeded. For a moment they tried to round them in again, and we were among them, and they did their best to check our advances, firing their guns and arrows. Some were armed only with the bow. One after another I saw four of them tumble from their horses to the ground, and the rest turned and fled in all directions, our party close after them. They outnumbered us, but perhaps our sudden and unexpected onslaught had demoralized them at the start. Somehow, the moment I rode out of the coulée and saw them, I felt no more fear, but instead became excited and anxious to be right at the front. I fired at several of them, but could not tell if they fell to my shots or those of our party. When they turned and fled I singled out one of them, a fellow riding a big strawberry pinto, and took after him. He made straight for Hairy Cap and its sheltering pines, and I saw at once that he had the better horse and would get away unless I could stop him with a bullet; and I fired shot after shot, each time thinking, "This time I must get him." Three times he loaded his flintlock and shot back at me. His aim must have been as bad as mine, for I never even heard the whiz of the bullets, nor saw them strike.

He had now reached the foot of the butte, and urged the horse up its steep side, soon reaching a point where it was so nearly perpendicular that the animal could carry him no farther. He jumped off and scrambled on up, leaving the horse. I also dismounted, knelt down, and, taking deliberate aim, fired three shots before he reached the pines. I saw the bullets strike, and not one of them was within ten feet of the fleeing mark. It was about the worst shooting I ever did.

Of course, I was not foolish enough to try to hunt the Indian in those thick pines, where he would have every advantage of me. His horse had run down the hill and out on the plain. I rode after it, and soon captured it. Riding back to the place where we had charged out of the coulée, I could see members of our party coming in from all directions, driving horses before them, and soon we were all together again. We had not lost a man and only one was wounded, a youth named Tail-feathers; an arrow had fearfully lacerated his right cheek, and he was puffed up with pride. Nine of the enemy had fallen, and sixty-three of their horses had been taken. Every one was jubilant over the result. Heavy Breast told me they were Crees.

We changed horses and turned homeward, plodding along steadily all that afternoon. The excitement was over, and the more I thought of it, the more pleased I was that I had not killed the Cree I chased into the pines. But the others—those I had fired at and seen drop—I succeeded in convincing myself that they were not my bullets that had caused them to fall. Had I not fired twenty shots at the man I chased, and each one wide of the mark? Of course, it was not I who laid them low. I had captured a fine horse, and I was satisfied.

We got home in four or five days, and there was great excitement over our arrival, and many a dance with the scalps by those who had at one time or another lost relatives at the hands of the Crees. Hands and faces and moccasins painted black, bearing the scalps on a willow stick, little parties went from one part of the village to another, singing the sad song of the dead, and dancing in step to its slow time.

Berry and his wife killed the fatted calf over my safe return; at least we had, besides choice meats and bread and beans, three dried apple pies and a plum (raisin) duff for dinner.

CHAPTER 5

Days with the Game

WHO should roll in one day but Sorrel Horse and his wife, with whom I had passed the summer, and with them came young Bear Head—once Wolverine—and his Gros Ventre wife, whom I had helped him steal from her people. Berry and his wife were as glad to meet them all again as I was, and gave them one of the rooms in the fort until such time as Sorrel Horse should have a cabin of his own. He had decided to winter with us, trap beaver and poison wolves, and perhaps do a little trading with the Indians. With Bear Head to help him, he soon built a comfortable two-room cabin just back of our place, and put in two good fireplaces like ours.

I had brought a shotgun west with me, and now that the geese and ducks were moving south, I had some very good shooting. Whenever I went out for a few birds a number of Indians always followed me to see the sport; they took as much delight in seeing a bird fall at the crack of the gun as I did in making the shot. Once I dropped eleven widgeons from a flock passing by, and the onlookers went wild with enthusiasm over it. But I could never induce them to accept any of the fowl I killed; birds and fish they would not eat, regarding the latter especially as unclean. All they cared for was ni-tap-i waksin: real food, by which was meant the meat of buffalo and the various other ruminants.

In November many of the Blackfeet came down from the
north, where they had been summering along the Saskatchewan and its tributaries, and following them came the Kai-na,
or Bloods, another tribe of the Blackfeet. The latter went into
camp a mile below the Piegans, and the former pitched their
lodges about half a mile above our fort. We now had, including
women and children, something like 9,000 or 10,000 Indians
about us, and the traders were kept busy all day long. Buffalo
robes were not yet prime but a fair trade was done in beaver,
elk, deer, and antelope skins. About the only groceries the
Indians bought were tea, sugar, and coffee, and they cost them,
on an average, one dollar per pint cupful. Blankets—three-
point—were twenty dollars; or four prime head and tail buffalo
robes, each; a rifle, costing fifteen dollars, sold for one hundred
dollars; whisky—very weak—was five dollars per quart, and
even a package of Chinese vermilion sold for two dollars. There
was certainly profit in the trade.

Winter came that year in the early part of November. The
lakes and streams froze over, there were several falls of snow,
which the northwest winds gathered up and piled in coulées
and on the lee side of the hills. It was not long before the buffalo
began to keep away from the river, where the big camps were.
A few, of course, were always straggling in, but the great herds
stayed out on the plains to the north and south of us. Since
the buffalo did not approach the stream the Indians were
obliged to go out on a two or three days' camping trip in order
to get what meat and skins they needed, and several times
during the season I went with them, accompanying my friends,
Weasel Tail and Talks-with-the-buffalo. On these short hunts
few lodges were taken, fifteen or twenty people arranging to
camp together, so we were somewhat crowded for room. Only
enough women to do the cooking accompanied the outfit.

As a rule, the hunters started out together every morning,
and sighting a large herd of buffalo, approached as cautiously
as possible, until finally the animals became alarmed and
started to run, and then a grand chase took place, and if everything was favorable many fat cows were killed. Nearly all the

Piegans had guns of one kind or another; either flintlock or percussion-cap, smooth-bore or rifle; but in the chase many of them, especially if riding swift, trained horses, preferred to use the bow and arrow, as two or three arrows could be discharged at as many different animals while one was reloading a gun. Some of the hunters killed twenty and more buffalo on a single run, but I think the average number to the man was not more than three.

When on these short hunts a medicine man always accompanied a party, and the evenings were passed in praying to the Sun for success in the hunt, and in singing songs, especially the song of the wolf, the most successful of hunters. Everyone retired early, for there was little cheer in a fire of buffalo chips.

By the latter end of November the trade for robes was in full swing, thousands of buffalo had been killed, and the women were busily engaged in tanning the hides, a task of no little labor. I have often heard and read that Indian women received no consideration from their husbands, and led a life of exceedingly hard and thankless work. That is very wide of the truth so far as the natives of the northern plains were concerned. It is true that the women gathered fuel for the lodge—bundles of dry willow, or limbs from a fallen cottonwood. They also did the cooking, and besides tanning robes, converted the skins of deer, elk, antelope, and mountain sheep into soft buckskin for family use. But when they felt like it they rested; they realized that there were other days coming, and they took their time about anything they had to do. Their husbands never interfered with them, any more than they did with him in his task of providing the hides and skins and meat, the staff of life. The majority—nearly all of them—were naturally industrious and took pride in their work, in putting away parfleche after parfleche of choice dried meats and pemmican, in tanning soft robes and buckskins for home use or sale, in embroidering wonderful patterns of beads or colored porcupine quills upon moccasin tops, dresses, leggings, and saddle trappings. When robes were to be traded they got their share of the proceeds; if the husband chose to buy liquor, well and good—they bought blankets and red and blue trade cloth, vermilion, beads, bright prints, and various other articles of use and adornment.

Berry and some of his men made several flying trips to Fort Benton during the winter, and on one of them brought out his mother, who had been living there with her companion, the Crow Woman. Mrs. Berry, Sr., was a full-blooded Mandan, but very light-colored, and brown-haired. She was tall and slender, good-looking, very proud and dignified, of great kindness of heart. She was very good to me, nursing me when ill and giving me strange and bitter medicines, always picking up and putting away with care the things I scattered about, washing and mending my clothes, making me beautiful moccasins and warm gloves. She could not have done more had she been my own mother; I was under obligation to her which nothing could ever repay. When I contracted mountain fever, and one evening became delirious, it was she who tended me, and brought me safely out of it. Her companion, the Crow Woman, was equally kind to me. She was a woman who had found a haven of peace and plenty with her good friend Mrs. Berry after a lifetime of surviving one bitter tribal war after another.

CHAPTER 6

A White Buffalo

ONE evening in the latter part of January there was much excitement in the three great camps. Some Piegan hunters, just returned from a few days' buffalo chase out on the plains to the north of the river, had seen a white buffalo. The news quickly spread, and from all quarters Indians came in to the post for powder and balls, flints, percussion caps, tobacco, and various other articles. There was to be an exodus of hunting parties from the three villages in the morning and men were betting with each other as to which of the tribes would secure the skin of the white animal; each one, of course, betting on his own tribe. By nearly all the tribes of the plains an albino buffalo was considered a sacred thing, the especial property of the Sun. When one was killed the hide was always beautifully tanned, and at the next medicine lodge was given to the Sun with great ceremony, hung above all the other offerings on the center post of the structure, and there left to shrivel gradually and fall to pieces. War parties of other tribes, passing the deserted place, would not touch it for fear of calling down upon themselves the wrath of the Sun. The man who killed such an animal was thought to have received the special favor of the Sun, and not only he, but his whole tribe.

A white robe was one thing which was never offered for sale; none who secured one might keep it any longer than until the time of the next medicine lodge, the great annual religious ceremony. Medicine men, however, were permitted to take the strips of trimming and use them for wrapping their sacred pipes, or for a bandage around the head—only to be worn, however, on great occasions.

I joined one of the hunting parties the next morning, going, as usual, with my friends, Talks-with-the-buffalo and Weasel Tail. We planned the hunt in the lodge of the latter, and as we might be some time away, it was decided to take one lodge and all its contents, and to allow no others to crowd in upon us. "That is," Weasel Tail added, "we'll do this, and take our wives along, too, if you think they will not get to quarreling about the right way to boil water, or as to the proper place to set an empty kettle."

His wife threw a moccasin at him, Madame Talks-with-the-buffalo pouted and exclaimed "K'yä!" and we all laughed.

We started early the next morning and never stopped until we arrived at a willow-bordered stream running out from the west butte of the Sweetgrass Hills and eventually disappearing in the dry plain. It was an ideal camping place—plenty of shelter, plenty of wood and water. The big herd with the albino buffalo had been last seen some fifteen miles southeast of our camp, and had run westward when pursued. Our party thought that we had selected the best location possible in order to scour the country in search of it. Those who had seen it reported that it was a fair-sized animal, and so swift that it had run up to the head of the herd at once and remained there—so far from their horses' best speed, that they never could determine whether it was bull or cow.

Other parties, Piegans, Blackfeet, and Bloods, were encamped east of us along the hills, and southeast of us out on the plain. We had agreed to do no running, to frighten the buffalo as little as possible until the albino had been found, or it became time to return to the river. Then, of course, a big run or two would be made in order to load the pack animals with meat and hides.

The weather was unfavorable, to say nothing of the intense

cold; a thick haze of glittering frost flakes filled the air, through which the sun shone dimly. We were almost at the foot of the west butte, but it and its pine forest had vanished in the shining frost fog. Nevertheless, we rode out daily on our quest, toward the Little River. We saw many buffalo; thousands of them, in bands of from twenty or thirty to four or five hundred, but we did not find the white one. Other parties often dropped in at our camp for a bite and a smoke, or were met out on the plain, and they had the same report to make: plenty of buffalo, but no albino. Antelope stood humped up in the biting cold; on the south slope of the butte, as we rode by its foot, we could see deer, and elk, and even big-horn in the same position. The latter would get out of our way, but the others hardly noticed our passing. Only the buffalo, the wolves, coyotes, seemed happy; the buffalo grazed about as usual, the others trotted around and feasted on the quarry they had hamstrung and pulled down, and howled and yelped throughout the long nights.

I cannot remember how many days that cold time lasted, during which we vainly hunted for the albino buffalo. The change came about ten o'clock one morning as we were riding slowly around the west side of the butte. We felt suddenly an intermittent tremor of warm air in our faces; the frost haze vanished instantly and we could see the Rockies, partially enveloped in dense, dark clouds. "Hah!" exclaimed a medicine-pipe man. "Did I not pray for a black wind last night? And see, here it is; my Sun power is strong."

Even as he spoke the chinook came on in strong, warm gusts and settled into a roaring, snapping blast. The thin coat of snow on the grass disappeared. One felt as if summer had come.

We were several hundred feet above the plain, on the lower slope of the butte, and in every direction, as far as we could see, there were buffalo, buffalo, and still more buffalo. They were a grand sight. Nature had been good to these Indians in providing for them such vast herds for their sustenance.

It seemed about as useless as looking for the proverbial needle to attempt to locate a single white animal among all those dark ones. We all dismounted, and, adjusting my long telescope, I searched herd after herd until my vision became blinded, and then I passed the instrument to someone beside me. Nearly all of the party tried it, but the result was the same; no white buffalo. We smoked and talked about the animal we were after; each one had his opinion as to where it was at that moment, and they varied in locality from the Missouri River to the Saskatchewan, from the Rockies to the Bear's Paw Mountains. While we were talking there appeared a commotion among the buffalo southeast of us. I got the telescope to bear upon the place and saw that a number of Indians were chasing a herd of a hundred or more due westward. They were far behind them, more than a mile, and the buffalo were widening that distance rapidly, but still the riders kept on in a long, straggling line. I passed the glass to Weasel Tail and told what I had seen. Everyone sprang to his feet.

"It must be," said my friend, "that they have found the white one, or they would give up the chase. They are far behind and their horses are tired. Yes, it is the white one they follow. I see it! I see it!"

We were mounted in a moment and riding out to intercept the herd; riding at a trot, occasionally broken by a short lope, for the horses must be kept fresh for the final run. In less than half an hour we arrived at a low, long, mound-like elevation, near which the herd should pass. We could see them coming straight toward it. So we got behind it and waited, my companions, as usual, removing their saddles and piling them in a heap. We realized, of course, that the buffalo might get wind of us and turn long before they were near enough for us to make a dash at them, but we had to take that chance. After a long time, our leader, peering over the top of the mound, told us to be ready; we all mounted. Then he called out for us to come on, and we dashed over the rise; the herd was yet over 500 yards distant, had winded us, and turned south. Whips were plied; short-handled quirts of rawhide which stung and maddened the horses. At first we gained rapidly on the herd, then for a time kept at about their speed, and finally began to lose distance. Still we kept on, for we could all see the coveted prize, the albino, running at the head of the herd. I felt sure that none of us could overtake it, but because the others did, I kept my horse going, too, shamefully quirting him when he was doing his best.

Then out from a coulée right in front of the flying herd dashed a lone horseman, right in among them, scattering the animals in all directions. In much less time than it takes to tell it, he rode up beside the albino. We could see him lean over and sink arrow after arrow into its ribs, and presently it stopped, wobbled, and fell over on its side. When we rode up to the place the hunter was standing over it, hands raised, fervently praying, promising the Sun the robe and the tongue of the animal. It was a three-year-old cow, yellowish-white in color, but with normal-colored eyes. The successful hunter was a Piegan, Medicine Weasel by name. He was so excited, he trembled so, that he could not use his knife, and some of our party took off the hide for him, and cut out the tongue, he standing over them all the time and begging them to be careful, to make no gashes, for they were doing the work for the Sun. None of the meat was taken. It was considered a sacrilege to eat it; the tongue was to be dried and given to the Sun with the robe. While the animal was being skinned, the party we had seen chasing the herd came up; they were Blackfeet of the north, and did not seem to be very well pleased that the Piegans had captured the prize; they soon rode away to their camp, and we went to ours, accompanied by Medicine Weasel.

CHAPTER 7

Winter on the Marias

THERE was a little town in northern Montana, where upon certain days things would run along as smoothly and monotonously as in a quiet Eastern village. But at certain other times you would enter the place to find everyone on a high old tear. It seemed to be epidemic; if one man started to get gloriously full everyone promptly joined in—doctor, lawyer, merchant, cattleman, sheepman and all. Well do I remember the last affair of that kind I witnessed there. By about 2 P.M. they got to the champagne stage—really sparkling cider at five dollars a bottle, and fifty men were going from saloon to store and from store to hotel treating in turn—sixty dollars a round. I mention this as a prelude to what I have to say about drinking among the Indians in the old days. They were no worse than the whites in that way, and with them it seemed to be also epidemic.

A camp would be quiet and orderly for days and days, and then suddenly all the men would start in on a drinking bout. True, they frequently quarreled with each other when in liquor, and a quarrel was something to be settled only by blood. But let a thousand white men get drunk together, and there would ensue some fearful scenes.

One night that winter on the Marias I was wending my way homeward from a visit at Sorrel Horse's place, when a man and woman came out of the trade room and staggered along the trail toward me. I slipped behind a cottonwood tree. The man was very unsteady on his feet and the woman, trying to help him along, at the same time was giving him a thorough scolding. I heard her say: "... and you didn't look out for me a bit; there you were in that crowd, just drinking with one and then another, and never looking to see how I was getting along. You don't protect me at all; you don't care for me, or you would not have let me stay in there to be insulted."

The man stopped short and, swaying this way and that, gave a roar like a wounded grizzly: "Don't care for you; don't protect you; let you get insulted," he spluttered and foamed. "Who insulted you? Who? I say. Let me at him! Let me at him! I'll fix him with this."

Right there by the trail was lying a large green cottonwood log which would have weighed at least a ton. He bent over it and tried again and again to lift it, shouting: "Protect you! Insulted! Who did it? Where is he? Wait until I pick up this club and let me at him."

But the club wouldn't be picked up, and he became perfectly frantic in his efforts to lift it up and place it on his shoulder. He danced from one end to the other of it with increasing anger, until he finally fell over it exhausted, and then the patient woman picked him up—he was a little, light fellow—and carried him home.

I knew a young man who always became very mischievous when he drank. He had three wives and at such times he would steal their little stores of fine pemmican, fancy bead-work, their needles and awls, and give them to other women. He was up to his pranks one morning as I happened along, and the women determined to catch and bind him until he became sober. But he would not be caught; they chased him through the camp, out toward the hills, by the river, back to camp, when, by means of a travois leaning against it, he climbed to the top of his lodge, seated himself in the V-shaped crotch of the lodge poles, and jibed the women for their poor running qualities, enumerated the articles he had stolen from them, and so on. He was exceedingly hilarious.

The wives held a whispered consultation, and one of them went inside. Their tormentor ceased jibing and began a drinking song:

> *Bear Chief, he gave me a drink,*
> *Bear Chief, he gave me a—*

That was as far as he got. The wife had thrown a huge armful of rye grass from her couch upon the smouldering fire, it blazed up with a sudden roar and burst of flame which reached the tenderest part of his anatomy; he gave a loud yell of surprise and pain and leaped from his perch. When he struck the ground the women were upon him and I know not how many lariats they coiled about him before they bore him inside amid the jeers and jests of a throng of spectators, and laid him upon his couch.

But there was another side, and by no means a pleasant one to this drinking business. Out on a hunt one day down on the Missouri, I killed a buffalo which had what the traders called a "beaver robe," because the hair was so exceedingly fine, thick, and of a glossy, silky nature. Beaver robes were rare, and I had skinned this with horns and hoofs intact. I wished to have it especially well tanned, as I intended it for a present to an Eastern friend. The Crow Woman, good old soul, declared that she would do the work herself, and promptly stretched the hide on a frame. The next morning it was frozen stiff as a board, and she was standing on it busily chipping it, when a half-drunk Cree came along. I happened in sight just as he was about to pull her off of the hide, and hurrying over there I struck him with all my power square in the forehead with my fist. The blow did not stagger him. The Cree picked up a broken lodge pole and came for me, and as I was unarmed I had to turn and ignominiously run; I was not so swift as my pursuer, either. It is hard to say what would have happened—probably

I would have been killed had Berry not seen the performance. The Cree was just on the point of giving me a blow on the head when Berry fired, and the Indian fell with a bullet through his shoulder. Some of his people came along and packed him home. Then the Cree chief and his council came over and we had a fine pow-wow about the matter. It ended by our paying damages. We did our best always to get along with as little friction as possible, but I did hate to pay that Cree for a wound he richly deserved.

We traded for several seasons with the Crees and North Blackfeet down on the Missouri. There was a certain young Blackfoot with whom I was especially friendly, but one day he came in very drunk and I refused to give him any liquor. He became very angry and walked out making dire threats. I had forgotten all about the incident when several hours later his wife came running in and said that Took-a-gun-under-the-water (It-su'-yi-na-makan) was coming to kill me. The woman was terribly frightened and begged me to pity her and not kill her husband, whom she dearly loved and who, when sober, would be terribly ashamed of himself for attempting to hurt me. I went to the door and saw my friend coming. He was naked except for his moccasins, and had painted his face, body, and limbs with fantastic stripes of green, yellow, and red; he was brandishing a .44 Winchester and calling upon the Sun to witness how he would kill me, his worst enemy. Of course I didn't want to kill him any more than his wife wished to see him killed. Terror-stricken, she ran and hid in a pile of robes, and I took my stand behind the open door with a Winchester. On he came, singing, shouting the war song, and saying repeatedly, "Where is that bad white man? Show him to me that I may give him one bullet, just this one little bullet?"

With carbine full cocked he strode in, looking eagerly ahead for a sight of me, and just as he passed I gave him a smart blow on top of the head with the barrel of my rifle; he dropped senseless to the floor, his carbine going off and sending the bullet through a case of tinned tomatoes on a shelf. The woman ran out from her hiding place at the sound of the shot, thinking that I had surely killed him; but her joy was great when she learned her mistake. Together we bound him tightly and got him home to his lodge.

Now, one often reads that an Indian never forgives an injury of any kind, no matter how much at fault he may have been. That is all wrong. The next morning Took-a-gun-under-the-water sent me a fine buffalo robe. At dusk he came in and begged me to forgive him. Ever after we were the best of friends. Whenever I had time for a short hunt back in the breaks, or out on the plains, I chose him for my companion, and a more faithful and considerate one I never had.

I cannot say that all traders got along so well with the Indians as did Berry and I. There were some bad men among them, men who delighted in inflicting pain, in seeing blood flow. I have known such to kill Indians just for fun, but never in a fair, open fight. They were great cowards, and utterly unprincipled. These men sold "whisky" which contained tobacco juice, cayenne pepper, snake heads and various other vile things. Berry and I sold weak liquor, it is true, but the weakness consisted of nothing but pure water—which was all the better for the consumer. There was but one redeeming feature about it: the trade was at a time when there was always more meat, more fur to be had for the killing of it. In comparison with various Government officials who robbed and starved the Indians to death on their reservations after the buffalo disappeared, we were saints.

Sometimes I would go with Sorrel Horse to visit his "baits," and it was a great sight to see the huge wolves lying stiff and stark about them. To make a good bait a buffalo was killed and cut open at the back, and into the meat, blood, and entrails three vials of strychnine—three-eighths of an ounce—were stirred. It seemed as if the merest bite of this deadly mixture was enough to kill, a victim seldom getting more than 200 yards away before the convulsions seized him. Of course, great numbers of coyotes and kit foxes were also poisoned, but they didn't count. The large, heavy-furred wolf skins were in great demand in the East for sleigh and carriage robes, and sold right at Fort Benton for from three dollars to five dollars each. I took some of these stiffly-frozen animals home, and stood them up around Sorrel Horse's house. They were an odd sight, standing there, heads and tails up, as if guarding the place; but one day there came a chinook wind and they soon toppled over and were skinned.

CHAPTER 8

I Have a Lodge of My Own

"WHY don't you get a woman?" Weasel Tail abruptly asked one evening as Talks-with-the-buffalo and I sat smoking with him in his lodge.

"Yes," my other friend put in. "Why not? You have the right to do so, for you can count a coup; yes, two of them. You killed a Cree, and you took a Cree horse in the fight at the Hairy Cap."

"I took a horse," I replied, "and a good one he is; but you are mistaken about the Cree; you will remember that he escaped by running into the pines on Hairy Cap."

"Oh!" said Talks-with-the-buffalo, "I don't mean that one; we all know he got away, I mean one of those who first fell when we all fired into them. That tall one, the man who wore a badger-skin cap; you killed him. I saw the bullet wound in his body; no ball from any of our rifles could have made such a small hole."

This was news to me; I remembered well having shot several times at that particular warrior, but I never had thought that my bullet ended his career. I did not know whether to feel glad or sorry about it, but finally concluded that it was best to feel glad, for he would have killed me if he could have done so. I was turning the matter over in my mind, when my host aroused me from my reverie: "I said, Why don't you take a woman? Answer."

"Oh!" I replied. "No one would have me. Isn't that a good reason?"

"Kyai-yo'!" exclaimed Madame Weasel Tail, clapping her hand to her mouth, the Blackfoot way of expressing surprise or wonder. "Kyai-yo'! What a reason! I well know that there isn't a girl in this camp but would like to be his woman. Why, if it wasn't for this lazy one here—" giving Weasel Tail's hand an affectionate squeeze—"if he would only go away somewhere and never come back, I'd make you take me. I'd follow you around until you would have to do so."

"Mah'-kah-kan-is-tsi!" I exclaimed, which is a flippant and slangy term, expressing doubt of the speaker's truthfulness.

"Mah'-kah-kan-is-tsi yourself," she rejoined. "Why do you think you are asked to all these Assiniboin dances, where all the young women wear their best clothes, and try to catch you with their robes? Why do you think they put on their best things and go to the trading post with their mothers or other relatives every chance they get? What, you don't know? Well, I'll tell you: they go, each one, hoping that you will notice her, and send a friend to her parents to make a proposal."

"It is the truth," said Weasel Tail.

"Yes, the truth," Talks-with-the-buffalo and his woman joined in.

I thought over the matter a good deal. All the long winter I had rather envied my good friends Berry and Sorrel Horse, who seemed to be so happy with their women. Never a cross word, always the best of good fellowship and open affection for each other. Seeing all this, I had several times said to myself: "It is not good that the man should be alone." The Blackfeet have much the same expression: "Mat'-ah-kwi täm-äp-i-ni-po-ke-mi-o-sin—not found (is) happiness without woman."

After that evening I looked more closely at the various young women I met in the camp or at the trading post, saying to myself: "Now, I wonder what kind of a woman that would make? Is she neat, good-tempered?" All the time, however, I knew that I had no right to take one of them. I did not intend to remain long in the West; my people would never forgive me for making an alliance with one. They were of old, proud Puritan stock, and I could imagine them holding up their hands in horror at the mere hint of such a thing.

"No," I said to myself: "no, it will not do; hunt, go to war, do anything but take a woman, and in the fall go home to your people." This is the line of conduct I meant to follow. But—

One morning the Crow Woman and I were sitting out under a shade she had constructed of a couple of travois and a robe or two. She was busy as usual, embroidering a moccasin with colored quills, and I was cleaning my rifle, preparatory to an antelope hunt. A couple of women came by on their way to the trade room with three or four robes. One of them was a girl of sixteen or seventeen; good-looking, fairly tall, and well-formed, she had fine large, candid, expressive eyes, white, even teeth and heavy braided hair which hung almost to the ground. "Who is that?" I asked the Crow Woman.

"Don't you know? She comes here often; she is a cousin of Berry's woman."

I went away on my hunt, but I was thinking all the time about the cousin. That evening I spoke to Berry about her; I learned that her father was dead; that her mother was a medicine lodge woman, and noted for her goodness of character. "I'd like to have the girl," I said. "What do you think about it?"

"We'll see," Berry replied. "I'll talk with my old woman."

A couple of days went by and nothing was said by either of us about the matter, and then one afternoon Mrs. Berry told me that I was to have the girl, providing I would promise to be always good and kind to her. I readily agreed to that.

"Very well, then," said Mrs. Berry; "go into the trade room and select a shawl, some dress goods, some bleached muslin— no, I'll select the outfit and make her some white women's dresses like mine."

"But hold on!" I exclaimed. "What am I to pay? How many horses, or whatever?"

"Her mother says there is to be no pay, only that you are to keep your promise to be good to her daughter."

Usually a lot of horses were sent to the parents, sometimes fifty or more. Sometimes the father demanded so many head, but if no number was specified, the suitor gave as many as he could. Again, it was not unusual for a father to request some promising youth, good hunter and bold raider, to become his son-in-law. In that case he was the one to give horses, and even a lodge and household goods, with the girl.

Well, I got the girl. It was an embarrassing time for us both when she came in one evening, shawl over her face, while we were eating supper. Sorrel Horse and his woman were there, and with Berry and his woman they made things interesting for us with their jokes, until Berry's mother put a stop to it. We were shy for a long time, she especially. "Yes" and "no" were about all that I could get her to say. But my room underwent a wonderful transformation; everything was kept so neat and clean, my clothes were so nicely washed, and my "medicine" was carefully taken out every day and hung on a tripod. I had purchased a war bonnet, shield, and various other things which the Blackfeet regard as sacred. I had them handled with due pomp and ceremony.

As time passed this young woman became more and more a mystery to me. I wondered what she thought of me, and if she speculated upon what I might think of her. I had no fault to find, she was always neat, always industrious about our little household affairs, quick to supply my wants. But that wasn't enough. I wanted to know her, her thoughts and beliefs. I wanted her to talk and laugh with me, and tell stories, as I could often hear her doing with the Berrys. Instead of that, when I came around, the laugh died on her lips, and she seemed to shrink within herself.

The change came when I least expected it. I was down in the Piegan camp one afternoon and learned that a war party was being made up to raid the Crows. Talks-with-the-buffalo and Weasel Tail were going, and asked me to go with them.

I readily agreed, and returned to the post to prepare for the trip.

"Nät-ah'-ki," I said, bursting into our room, "give me all the moccasins I have, some clean socks, some pemmican. Where is my little brown canvas bag? Where have you put my gun case? Where—"

"What are you going to do?"

It was the first question she had ever asked me.

"Do? I'm going to war; my friends are going, they asked me to join them—"

I stopped, for she suddenly arose and faced me, and her eyes were very bright. "You are going to war!" she exclaimed. "You, a white man, are going with a lot of Indians sneaking over the plains at night to steal horses, and perhaps kill some poor prairie people. You have no shame!"

"Why," I said, rather faintly, "I thought you would be glad. Are not the Crows your enemies? I have promised, I must go."

"It is well for the Indians to do this," she went on, "but not for a white man. You, you are rich; you have everything you want; those papers, that yellow hard rock (gold) you carry will buy anything you want; you should be ashamed to go sneaking over the plains like a coyote. None of your people ever did that."

"I have given my promise to go."

Then Nät-ah'-ki began to cry, and she came nearer and grasped my sleeve. "Don't go," she pleaded, "for if you do, I know you will be killed, and I love you so much."

I was never so surprised. All these weeks of silence, then, had been nothing but a veil to cover her feelings. I was pleased and proud to know that she did care for me, but underlying that though was another one: I had done wrong in taking this girl, in getting her to care for me, when in a short time I must return her to her mother and leave for my own country.

I readily promised not to accompany the war party, and then, her point gained, Nät-ah'-ki suddenly felt that she had been over-bold and tried to assume her reserve again. But I would not have it that way. I grasped her hand and made her sit down by my side, and pointed out to her that she was wrong; that to laugh, to joke, to be good friends and companions was better than to pass our days in silence, repressing all natural feeling. After that, the sun always shone.

CHAPTER 9

The Killing of a Bear

TOWARD the end of April we abandoned the trading post. Berry intended to resume freighting to the mines as soon as the steamboats began to arrive, and moved his family to Fort Benton. There also went Sorrel Horse and his outfit. The Bloods and Blackfeet moved north to summer on the Belly and Saskatchewan rivers. Most of the Piegans trailed over to Milk River and the Sweetgrass Hills country. The band with which I was connected, the Small Robes, pulled out for the foot of the Rockies, and I went with them. I had purchased a lodge and half a dozen pack and train animals to transport our outfit. We had a Dutch oven, two fry pans, a couple of small kettles, and some tin and iron tableware, of which Nät-ah'-ki was very proud. Our commissary consisted of one sack of flour, some sugar, salt, beans, coffee, bacon, and dried apples. I had plenty of tobacco and cartridges. We were rich; the world was before us. When the time came to move, I attempted to help pack our outfit, but Nät-ah'-ki stopped me at once.

"Aren't you ashamed?" she said. "This is my work; you go up in front there and ride with the chiefs. I'll attend to this."

After that I rode ahead with the big men, or hunted along by the way, and at evening on arriving at camp there was our lodge set up, a pile of fuel beside it, a bright fire within, over which the evening meal was being prepared. The girl and her mother had done it all, and when everything was in order the latter went away to the lodge of her brother, with whom she lived. We had many visitors, and I was constantly being asked to go and feast and smoke with this one and that one. Our stores of provisions did not last long, and we soon were reduced to a diet of straight meat. Every one was contented with that but I; how I did long at times for an apple pie, or some potatoes. I often dreamed that I was the happy possessor of some candy.

Leaving the abandoned fort, we followed up the Marias, then its most northern tributary, the Cutbank River, until we came to the pines at the foot of the Rockies. Here was game in vast numbers; not many buffalo nor antelopes just there, but elk, deer, mountain sheep and moose were even more plentiful than I had seen them south of the Missouri. As for bears, the whole country was torn up by them. None of the women would venture out after fuel or poles for lodge or travois without an escort. Many of the hunters never molested a grizzly, the bear being regarded as a sort of medicine or sacred animal, many believing that it was really a human being. It was commonly called Kyai'-yo, but the medicine-pipe men were obliged when speaking of it to call it Pah'-ksi-kwo-yi, sticky mouth. They, too, were the only ones who could take any of the skin of a bear, and then merely a strip for a head band or pipe wrapping. It was allowable, however, for anyone to use the bear's claws for a necklace or other ornament. Some of the more adventurous wore a three or four-row necklace of their own killing, of which they were very proud.

One morning with Heavy Breast I went up on the divide between Cutbank and Milk River for meat. We shot two prime bighorn rams, packed them on our horses and started homeward. Passing out of the pines we saw, some four or five hundred yards distant, a large grizzly industriously tearing up the sod on the bare hillside, in search of a gopher, or an ants' nest.

"Let us kill him," I exclaimed.

"Ok-yi (come on)," said Heavy Breast, but with an inflection which meant, "All right, but it's your proposition, not mine."

We rode along in the edge of the timber down under the hill, my companion praying, promising the Sun an offering, and begging for success. At the foot of the hill we turned into a deep coulée and followed it up until we thought we were near the place where we had seen the bear; then we rode up out of it, and there was the old fellow not fifty yards away. He saw us as quickly as we did him, sat up on his haunches and wiggled his nose as he sniffed the air. We both fired and with a hair-lifting roar the bear rolled over, biting and clawing at his flank where a bullet had struck him, and then springing to his feet he charged us open-mouthed. We both urged our horses off to the north, for it was not wise to turn back down the hill. I fired a couple of shots as fast as I could, but without effect. The bear meantime had covered the ground with surprisingly long bounds, and was already close to the heels of my companion's horse. I fired again and made another miss, and just then Heavy Breast, his saddle, and his sheep meat parted company with the fleeing pony; the cinch, an old, worn, rawhide band, had broken.

"Hai ya', my friend!" he cried, pleadingly, as he soared up in the air, still astride the saddle. Down they came with a loud thud not two steps in front of the onrushing bear, and that animal, with a dismayed and frightened "woof," turned sharply about and fled back toward the timber, I after him. I kept firing, and finally a lucky shot broke his backbone; it was easy then to finish him with a deliberately aimed bullet in the base of the brain. When it was over I suddenly remembered how ridiculous Heavy Breast had appeared soaring on a horseless saddle, and how his eyes bulged as he called upon me for aid. I began to laugh and it seemed as if I never could stop. My companion had come up beside me and stood, very solemn, looking at me and the bear.

"Do not laugh, my friend," he said. "Do not laugh. Rather, pray to the good Sun, make sacrifice to him, that when you are sometime hard pressed by the enemy, or such another one as he lying here, you may as fortunately escape as did I. Surely the Sun listened to my prayer. I promised to sacrifice to him, intending to hang up that fine white blanket I have just bought. I will now do better. I will hang up the blanket and my otter-skin cap."

The bear had a fine coat of fur, and I determined to take it and have it tanned. Heavy Breast took my horse in order to catch his, which had run out of sight into the valley, and I set to work. It was no small task, for the bear was quite fat, and I wanted to get the hide off as clean as possible. Long before I accomplished it my friend returned with his animal, dismounted a little way off, sat down, filled and lighted his pipe.

"Help me," I said, after he had smoked. "I'm getting tired."

"I cannot do so," said he. "It is against my medicine; my dream forbade me to touch a bear."

We arrived in camp finally, and hearing me ride up beside the lodge, Nät-ah'-ki hurried out.

"Kyai-yo'!" she exclaimed, and hurried back inside.

I thought that rather strange, for when I came in from a hunt she always insisted upon unpacking and unsaddling my mount, and leading the animal over to the lodge of a boy who took care of my little band. After I had done this I went inside; a dish of boiled boss ribs, a bowl of soup were ready for me. As I ate I told about the day's hunt, but when I described how Heavy Breast had sailed through the air and how he looked when he cried out to me, Nät-ah'-ki did not laugh with me. I thought that strange, also, for she was so quick to see the comical side of things.

"It is a fine hide," I concluded; "long, thick, dark hair. I wish you would tan it for me."

"Ah!" she exclaimed, "I knew you would ask that as soon as I saw it. Have pity on me, for I cannot do it. I cannot touch it. Only here and there is a woman, or even a man, who through the power of their medicine can handle a bear skin. To others who attempt it some great misfortune befalls; sickness, even death. None of us here would dare to tan the skin. There is a woman of the Kut-ai'-im-iks (Do-not-laugh-band) who would do it for you, another in the Buffalo-chip band; yes, there are several, but they are all far away."

I said no more about it, and after a while went out and stretched the skin, by pegging it to the ground. Nät-ah'-ki was uneasy, repeatedly coming out to watch me for a moment, and then hurrying inside again. I kept at work; there was still a lot of fat on the skin; try as I would I could not get it all off. I was pretty greasy and tired of my job when night came.

I awoke soon after daylight. Nät-ah'-ki was already up and out. I could hear her praying near the lodge, telling the Sun that she was about to take the bearskin, flesh and tan it. She begged her God to have mercy on her; she did not want to; she feared to touch the unclean thing, but her man wished it to be worked into a soft robe.

"Oh, Sun!" she concluded, "help me, protect me, from the evil power of the shadow of this bear. I will sacrifice to you. Let my good health continue, give us all, my man, my mother, my relatives, me, give us all long life, happiness; let us live to be old."

My first thought was to call and say that she need not tan the skin, that I really did not care for a bear robe after all; but I concluded that it would be well for her to do the work. If she did not learn that there was nothing in the malevolent influence of the bear's spirit, she would at least beget confidence in herself and her medicine. So I lay still for a while, listening to the quick chuck-chuck of her flesher as it stripped meat and fat from the skin. After a little she came in, and seeing that I was awake, built a fire for the morning meal. As soon as it began to burn she washed herself in half a dozen waters, and then, placing some dried sweetgrass on a few live coals, she bent over its fragrant smoke, rubbing her hands in it.

"What are you doing?" I asked. "Why burning sweetgrass this early?"

"I purify myself," she replied. "I am fleshing the bearskin. I am going to tan it for you."

"Now, that is kind," I told her. "When we go to Fort Benton I will get you the prettiest shawl I can find, and is there any sacrifice to be made? Tell me, that I may furnish it."

The woman was pleased. She smiled happily, and then became very serious. Sitting down by my side she bent over and whispered:

"I have prayed. I have promised a sacrifice for you and for me. We must give something good. You have two short guns; can you not spare one? and I, I will give my blue cloth dress."

The blue cloth dress, her most cherished possession, seldom worn but often taken from its parfleche covering, smoothed out, folded, refolded, admired, and then put away again. Surely, if she could part with that I could afford to lose one of my six-shooters. One of them—they were the old Colt cap-and-ball affairs—had a trick of discharging all the chambers at once. Yes, I would give that. So, after breakfast we went out a little way from camp and hung our offerings in a tree, Nät-ah'-ki praying while I climbed up and securely fastened them to a sturdy branch. All that day women of the camp came and stared at the tanner of the bearskin, some begging her to quit the work at once, all prophesying that she would in some way have bad luck. But she kept on, and in the course of four or five days I had a large, soft, bear rug with which I promptly covered our couch. But there it seemed it could not remain if I cared to have any visitors, for none of my friends would enter the lodge while it was inside. I was obliged to store it away under a couple of rawhides behind our home.

We remained on the Cutbank River until about the first of June. The flies were becoming troublesome and we moved out on the plains where they were not nearly so plentiful. Swinging over the ridge we went down the course of Milk River, finally camping just north of the Sweetgrass Hills, where the rest of the Piegans were staying. There was much coming and going of visitors between the two camps. We learned that a great scandal had occurred in the Do-not-laugh band soon after leaving the Marias. Yellow Bird Woman, the young and pretty wife of old Looking Back, had run away with a youth named Two Stars. It was thought that they had gone north to the Bloods or Blackfeet, and the husband had started in pursuit of them.

There was much talk about the affair, much conjecture as to what would be the end of it.

One evening Nät-ah'-ki informed me that the guilty couple had arrived from the north, and were in the lodge of a young friend of theirs. They had eluded the husband when he arrived in the Blood camp, and doubled back south. He would probably go on to the Blackfoot camp in search of them, and they, meanwhile, were going on to visit the Gros Ventres. After a time they hoped he would give up the chase, and then, by paying him heavy damages, they would be allowed to live together in peace. The very next morning, however, soon after sunrise, our camp was aroused by a woman's piercing, terror-stricken shrieks. Everyone sprang from bed and ran out, the men with their weapons, thinking that perhaps some enemy was attacking us. But it was Yellow Bird Woman who shrieked; her husband had found and seized her as she was going to the stream for water, he had her by one wrist and was dragging her to the lodge of our chief, the woman hanging back, crying and struggling to get loose. Breakfast was prepared in the lodges, but that morning the camp was very quiet. There was no singing, no laughter, no talking. I remarked upon it to my woman.

"Hush," she said, "she is to be pitied; I think something dreadful is about to happen."

Presently we heard the camp-crier shouting out that there was to be a council in Big Lake's lodge, and he called over the names of those requested to be present; medicine-pipe men, mature hunters and warriors, wise old men. One by one they went over to the place; a profound silence settled over the camp.

We had our breakfast when the camp-crier was again heard: "All women! all women!" he shouted. "You are to assemble at once at the lodge of our chief, where a punishment is about to take place. You are to witness what happens to a woman who disgraces her husband, her relatives, and herself."

I imagine that few women wanted to go, but following the camp-crier were the Crazy Dog band of all the All Friends Society, camp police, who went from lodge to lodge and ordered the women out. As one raised the flap of our doorway Nät-ah'-ki sprang over to me and grasped me convulsively.

"Come," said the policeman, looking in. "Come, hurry! Didn't you hear the call?"

"She is no longer a Piegan," I said quietly, although I felt angry enough. "She is a white woman now, and she does not go."

I thought there might be some argument about the matter, but there was none; the man dropped the door flap and went away without a word.

We waited in suspense. "What are they going to do?" I asked. "Kill her or—the other thing?"

Nät-ah'-ki shuddered and did not answer, clinging to me more closely than ever. Suddenly we heard again those piercing shrieks; then again all was silence until our chief began to talk.

"Kyi!" he said. "You all here standing, have witnessed what befalls one who proves untrue to her husband. It is a great crime, unfaithfulness. In the long ago our fathers counseled together as to what should be the punishment of a woman who brought sorrow and shame to the lodge of her man and her parents. And as they decided should be done, so has it been done to this woman today that all you witnessing it may take warning. She is marked with a mark she will bear as long as she lives. Wherever she goes people will look and laugh and say: 'Ha, a cut-nosed woman! There goes a woman of loose character; isn't she pretty?' "

Then, one after another, several men made little speeches, each one to the same effect, and when they had finished the chief told the people to disperse. The woman went to the river to wash her bleeding face; from the bridge to the lip her nose had been entirely removed with one deep concaved slash. She was a horrible sight, an animated human skull.

The youth had hurried away to his own camp and lodge as soon as the woman was caught. Nothing was said or done to him.

CHAPTER 10

The Kutenai Arrive

IT was after breakfast. Nät-ah'-ki recombed and rebraided her hair, binding it with a bright blue ribbon, donned her best dress, put on her prettiest pair of moccasins.

"Why all this finery?"

"This morning Lone Elk takes out his sacred pipe, carrying it about through the camp. We follow him. Will you come?"

Of course I would go, and I also put on my finery, a pair of fringed buckskin trousers, with bright, beaded vine-work running along the outer seams; a fringed and beaded buckskin shirt, a pair of gorgeous moccasins and my hair so long that it rippled down over my shoulders. Many a time, in speaking of the old days, various factors of the American Fur Company said, "Yes, he was a chief; he wore long hair. There are no more white chiefs; all those we now meet are sheared."

There was such a crowd around the lodge of the medicine man that we could not get near it, but the lodge skin was raised all around and we could see what was going on. With hands purified by the smoke of burning sweetgrass, Lone Elk was removing the wrappings of the sacred pipestem; singing, he and those seated in the lodge, the appropriate song for each wrap. At last the long stem—eagle-plumed, fur-wrapped, with tufts of brilliant feathers, lay exposed—and reverently lifting it he held it up toward the sun, down toward the earth, pointed it to the north, south, east, and west as he prayed for health, happiness, long life for all of us. Then rising, and holding the stem extended in front of him he danced slowly, deliberately out of the lodge, the men, I too, falling in one by one behind him. So did the women and the child, until there were several hundred of us in the long, snakelike procession, dancing along, weaving in and out round the lodges of the camp, singing the various songs of the medicine pipe. A song finished; we rested a little before another one was started, and in the interval the people talked and laughed. They were happy; not one there but believed in the efficacy of their prayers and devotion; that the Sun was pleased to see them there, dressed in their very best, dancing in his honor. Thus we went on until the whole circuit of the camp had been made and our leader came to the doorway of his lodge; there he dismissed us and we went home to resume our everyday clothing and occupations.

In June three Kutenai Indians came to our camp, bringing to Big Lake some tobacco from their chief and the proposal of a visit of his tribe to the Piegans. They had come straight to us from their country across the Rockies, up through the forests of the western slope, over the glacier-capped heights of the mountains, down the deep cañon of Cutbank Stream, and then straight to our camp, a hundred miles out in the vast plain. How could they find the way to the only camp in all that immense stretch of mountain and butte-sentineled, rolling plain? They may have struck the trail of some homing war party, some marauding party of their own people may have given them the location of those they sought. Anyhow, straight to us they came from the headwaters of the Columbia, and our chiefs took the tobacco they brought, smoked it in council, and pronounced it good. Some who had lost relatives in war against the mountain tribe objected to making peace with them, and talked earnestly against it. But the majority were against them, and the messengers departed with word to their chief that the Piegans would be glad to have a long visit from him and his people.

In due time they came, no more than seven hundred all told, which, I understood, was the larger part of the tribe. They were very different physically from the Piegans, much heavier built, with larger hands and feet. This was the result of their mountain life; they were great big-horn and goat hunters, and constant climbing had developed their leg muscles almost abnormally. The Blackfeet disdained that sort of life; they would not hunt game they could not ride to, and the hardest work they ever did was to butcher the animals they killed and pack the meat on the horses. No wonder, then, that their hands and feet were small and delicately fashioned, the former as soft and smooth as those of a woman.

Old Sah'-aw-ko-kin-ap-i, Back-in-sight, the Kutenai chief, came on with a few of his head men in advance of the main body, and before our chief Big Lake was aware that the expected visitors were anywhere near, the door-flap of his lodge was raised and the Kutenais entered. Taken by surprise, it was customary for the host to make the visitor a present, and by the end of the first smoke the Kutenai chief was five horses richer than when he entered the camp.

The Kutenais pitched their lodges close by our camp and before the women fairly got them up and fires burning, visiting and feasting and exchanging presents between the two tribes was in full swing. The Kutenais brought with them large quantities of arrowroot and dried camas, the latter a yellow, sweet, sticky, roasted bulb which tasted good to one who had not seen a vegetable of any kind for months. The Piegans were exceedingly pleased to get these, and in return gave the Kutenai wives much of their choice pemmican and dried meats, and they bartered buffalo leather and parfleche for the tanned skins of sheep and moose.

Of course the young men of both tribes went courting. In the Kutenai camp were the Piegan youths, and vice versa, standing in silent stateliness, decked out in all their gorgeous finery, their faces strikingly painted, their long hair neatly braided. The more fortunate of them carried suspended by a thong from the left wrist a small mirror which kept turning and flashing in the bright sunlight; sometimes the mirror was set into a rude wooden frame carved by the owner and brightly painted. Of course these gallants never spoke to any of the maidens about, nor could one be sure that they even looked at them. They stood by the hour, apparently gazing away at some distant object, but on the sly they were really watching the girls, and knew intimately every feature of each one's face, every little trait of action and repose. The maids were apparently wholly unaware that there were any young men in the camp. But they would get together and discuss the looks of this one and that one, and his valor, and temper, just as do white girls. Nät-ah'-ki told me all about it, and how, in secret, they ridiculed and laughed at some vainglorious swain who did not please them, but who thought himself the only perfect beau of the camp.

There was much racing, gambling and dancing by the younger men of the two camps. Their elders looked on at it all in quiet approval, and talked of their hunts and battles, and the strange places and things they had seen.

The Kutenais owned a large, clean-limbed and very swift black mare which, with one horse after another, the Piegans had endeavored to beat. Race after race had been run and each time the black had been victorious. The Piegans had lost heavily—guns, horses, blankets, finery of all descriptions—and were getting desperate. They claimed, for one thing, that the winners had managed secretly to rub something on their horses which reduced the speed of the animals. They decided to send over to the Bloods for a certain horse which was known to be very fast, and to guard him night and day until the race was run.

The deputation returned with the horse, a fine well-blooded American bay which had undoubtedly been taken from some unfortunate traveler on the Overland trail far to the south. He was to rest four days, and then the great race was to be run in which the Piegans expected to recoup their losses. By day half a dozen young men guarded him out on the plain, where he grazed upon the richest grass that could be found, and at night he was fairly surrounded by interested watchers.

At last the great day came, and everyone in both camps, even the women and children, went out to the level stretch about 500 yards long. The betting was furious, and more stuff was set out here and there on the plain than I ever saw before or since. Specimens of everything the two tribes had for use or adornment were to be found in one or another of the heaps, and the many horses which had been staked upon the result were also there, their ropes held by some non-betting boy. Even the women were betting; here you would see a brass kettle wagered against a beaded dress, there a parfleche of dried buffalo meat against a tanned elkskin, a yard of red cloth against a couple of copper bracelets. I stood with a crowd of others at the finishing point, where a furrow had been scraped across the dusty course.

It was to be a standing start; we could see the two youthful riders, naked except for breech-clouts, guide their excited mounts up to the starting point. They were off; the spectators lining the course began to shout, encouraging the riders to do their utmost, an increasing confusion and clamor of Blackfoot and Kutenai exclamations, with the shrill cries of the women. We at the post could not tell which horse was ahead, as they came toward us with quick, long leaps; they seemed to be running side by side. Now, as they neared the goal, a sudden silence fell upon the crowd. We could hear the riders' quirts thwack against the straining sides of the racers. And now here they were; a few leaps more and they crossed the furrow almost neck and neck, the Kutenai horse, I thought, a few inches in the lead. Immediately a great clamor arose and there was a general rush for the stakes.

"We win!" the Piegans shouted, "We win!" and I presume that is what the Kutenais were saying in their angry words. There was a confused rush to the stakes. Men pulled and pushed each other for possession of them. A Kutenai in the midst of a struggling group pulled an ancient flintlock pistol and aimed it at his opponent, but someone knocked it upward, and the bullet went wide. At the sound of the shot the women fled in terror to their lodges, dragging their crying children after them. The hot-headed Piegan men began to call to each other: "Get your weapons! Let us kill off all of these Kutenai cheats."

There was no more struggling over the things which had been staked upon the result of the race. Each bettor seemed to take that which was his without protest and hurry away to his lodge. In a moment the race ground was deserted save by the Kutenai and Piegan chiefs, a few of their leading men, Nät-ah'-ki and I. The latter was grasping my arm and there was real terror in her eyes as she begged me to go with her at once.

"There is going to be a big fight; let us saddle our horses and ride away from it," she said. "Come."

"The fight will not concern me," I told her. "I am a white man."

"Yes," she cried, "you are a white man, and you are also a Piegan; the Kutenais will shoot at you as quickly as at anyone else."

I motioned her to keep silent, for I wanted to hear what was being decided upon by the chiefs. Big Lake sent his camp crier home.

"Tell them," he said, "that I go now to the camp of my good friend Back-in-sight; whoever would fight the Kutenais must fight me and these here with me."

The crier hurried away and then he turned to me. "Come," he said, "you also are for peace; come with us."

I went with them over to the Kutenai camp, Nät-ah'-ki, sorely troubled, following. We barely arrived there when we saw an increasing throng of shouting and excited riders bearing down upon us from the other camp.

"Loan me a gun," said Big Lake, peremptorily. "Someone loan me a gun."

When it was handed him he stepped out in front of us and there was a look of grim determination on his fine old face, an angry light in his eyes. Behind us, with rustle of lodge-skin and rattle of poles, the lodges were being hurriedly taken down, the baggage packed by anxious women, and near us the Kutenai men were preparing to defend themselves and theirs. They were no match for the Piegans, they well knew; they were far outnumbered; but one had only to look at their attitude of preparedness, their steady eyes and compressed lips, to be satisfied that they would do their best.

A young warrior named Little Deer was at the head of the Piegans as they came riding fast toward us. I had a strong dislike to him, for I felt that he hated me. He had a mean, cruel face, pitiless and treacherous, with shifty eyes. Big Lake hastened out to meet them, shouting to them, and making the sign for them to stop. But as they paid no heed he ran on, and leveling his gun at Little Deer, exclaimed: "If you don't stop I will shoot."

The latter unwillingly checked his horse and said: "Why do you stop me? These Kutenai dogs have robbed us, cheated us; we are going to have revenge."

He started to go on, calling out to his followers, and again Big Lake raised his gun: "Aim then at me," he cried, "I am now a Kutenai. Aim, shoot; I give you a chance."

Little Deer did not raise his gun; he just sat there on his horse and glared at the chief, then turned in his saddle and looking at the crowd which had ridden up behind him, called upon them to follow him. But the other Piegan leaders were now among them, by turns threatening and coaxing them to return to their camp. None of them came forward; on the other hand, some started back toward their lodges. Little Deer worked himself into a fine rage, alternately pointing at them and at the Kutenais, calling them all the evil names he could think of. But in spite of his anger and defiance he made no attempt to advance; the chief's pointed gun, the steady cold, clear stare of his eyes wholly disconcerted him. Muttering something unintelligible, he finally turned his horse and moodily rode back to camp in the wake of those whom but a few moments before he had so eagerly led. The chiefs gave a long sigh of relief; so did I, so did Nät-ah'-ki, again close by my side.

"What hard heads these young men have," Big Lake remarked. "How difficult it is to manage them."

"You speak truth," said Back-in-sight. "Were it not for you, your strong words, many dead would now be lying on this plain. We go now back to the mountains; it may be long ere we meet again."

"Yes," agreed the Piegan, "it is best that we part. But the anger of our young men will soon die away. Next summer, somewhere hereabouts, let us meet again."

This was agreed upon, and with final handshakes all around, we left them. Arrived at our own camp, Big Lake gave orders that camp be struck at once, and the lodges began to come down in a hurry. He also instructed the Ai-in'-ai-kiks—police— to allow none of the young men to leave us under any pretext whatever. He feared that if they did go from us they would attack the Kutenais, who were already stringing out in a long column, westward over the rolling plain. A little later we too pulled out, heading south.

CHAPTER 11

The Snake Woman

THE day after we went into camp on the Marias, there was to be a buffalo run out on the flat beyond the Medicine Rock, where an immense herd had been located. Weasel Tail and I, however, chose to go up the Dry Fork on discovery. In our lodges were many a parfleche of dried meat; we wanted no summer skins of the buffalo, and, of course, we could kill what fresh meat was needed at almost any time and place. We crossed the river and rode through the bottom, then followed a broad, deep game trail running up the narrow valley of the Dry Fork, crossing and recrossing the stream.

By noontime we were well up the Dry Fork, twelve or fourteen miles from camp. Off to our right was a long ridge running east and west, the nearer point of it broken by sandstone cliffs. Arrived at the foot of the ridge, we picketed our horses and climbing up, sat down on its crest to get a view of the country. I had brought some broiled antelope ribs, and, opening the little bag, laid them upon a convenient rock. "Take part of them," I said.

Weasel Tail shook his head. "It is not wise," he replied, "to eat when out on discovery, on the hunt, or when traveling anywhere away from camp. You eat and rest, as lazy and sleepy as a full-gorged bear, and toward evening you arise and go homeward, finding no game whatever by the way. You arrive at your lodge, the people see that you bring neither meat nor skins. Your women quietly unsaddle your horse; you go inside and sit down upon your couch, much ashamed, and begin to lie, telling how very far you have ridden, how barren the country is, and how you wonder where the game can be.

"No, friend, no ribs for me. You eat, if you will. Loan me your glass and I will have a look at the country."

What Weasel Tail said was all very true. But this time need not count. I ate most of the meat, joined my friend in a smoke, and fell asleep.

Weasel Tail poked me in the ribs several times and I sat up and rubbed my eyes. My throat felt dry; there was a fuzzy taste in my mouth all caused by my midday lunch and nap. The sun was down toward the distant blue peaks of the Rockies. My friend was looking steadily through the glass to the westward and muttering to himself.

"It does not seem possible," he replied, "that I see that which I see; yet, I am sure neither my eyes nor this glass deceive. I see a woman; a lone woman, a woman on foot walking along the crest of the ridge yonder and coming straight toward us."

"Let me look," I exclaimed, dropping the pipe and taking the glass. "Are you sure you are awake?"

"See for yourself," he replied. "She is on the third rise from here."

I brought the glass to bear on the slope indicated, and, sure enough, there was a woman striding easily down the grassy incline. She stopped, turned, and shading her eyes with her hand, looked away to the south, then to the north, and lastly back whence she had come. I noticed that she carried a small pack on her back, that she stood erect, and was of slender figure. A young woman, undoubtedly. But why was she there, and afoot on that great plain whose vastness and silence must be appalling to one so alone and so defenseless.

"What do you think of this?" I asked.

"I don't think anything," Weasel Tail replied. "It is useless to try to account for so strange a thing. She comes this way; we will meet, and she will tell us the reason of it all."

The woman passed out of sight into the hollow back of the second rise of the ridge, but soon appeared on its crest and kept on down into the next low place. When she arrived at the top of the slope on which we sat, she saw us at once, stopped and hesitated for an instant, and then came on with her natural, easy, graceful stride. There was neither fear nor diffidence in her manner, as she walked steadily up to us. My first impression was that she had beautiful eyes; large, clear, kindly, honest eyes, and my next was that her face was exceedingly comely, her long hair glossy and neatly braided, her figure all that one expects a woman's form to be. She came on, quite up to us, and said: "How?"

"How, how?" we answered.

She unslung her pack, sat down, and began to talk in a language unintelligible to us. By signs we interrupted and said that we did not understand her talk.

"She is a Snake woman," said Weasel Tail. "By the cut and pattern of her moccasins I know that she is one of that tribe.

"Who are you?" Weasel Tail asked, "and whence come you?"

"I am a Snake," the woman signed, "and I come from the camp of my people far to the south." For a moment or two she sat thinking, brow wrinkled, lips pursed, and then continued:

"Three winters ago I became Two Bears' woman. He was very handsome, very brave, kind-hearted. I loved him, he loved me; we were happy." Again she paused, and tears rolled down her cheeks. She brushed them away repeatedly, and with much effort resumed her story: "We were very happy for he never got angry; no one ever heard cross words in our lodge. It was a lodge of feasts, and song, and laughter. Daily we prayed to the Sun, asking him to continue our happiness, to let us live long.

"It was three moons ago, two before this one which is almost ended. Winter had gone, the grass and leaves were coming out. I awoke one morning and found that I was alone in the lodge.

My chief had arisen while I slept; he had taken his gun, his saddle and rope, so I knew that he had started on a hunt. I was glad. 'He will bring home meat,' I said, 'fat meat of some kind, and we will give a feast.' I gathered wood, I got water, and then I sat down to await his return. All day I sat in the lodge waiting for him, sewing moccasins, listening for the footfalls of his hunting horse. The sun went down, and I built a good fire. 'He will come soon now,' I said.

"But no, he did not come, and I began to feel uneasy. Far into the night I sat waiting, and fear pressed harder and harder on my heart. Soon the people of the village went to bed. I arose and went to my father's lodge, but I did not sleep.

"When morning came the men rode out to look for my chief; all day they hunted through the little prairies, through the forests, along the river, but they did not find him, nor any signs of him, nor of his horse. For three days they rode the country in all directions, and then gave up. 'He is dead,' they said; 'he has drowned, or a bear or some enemy has killed him. It must have been an enemy, else his horse would have returned to its mates.'

"My own thought was that he lived; I could not believe him dead. My mother told me to cut off my hair, but I would not do it. I said to her: 'He is alive. When he returns should he find my long hair gone he will be angry, for he loves it. Many a time he has himself combed and braided it.'

"The days passed and I waited, waited and watched for him to come. I began to think that he might be dead, and then one night my dream gave me hope. The next night and the next it was the same, and then on the fourth night, when my dream again came and told me I knew that it was true, that he lived. 'Far away to the north,' said my dream, 'on a river of the plains, your chief lies wounded and ill in a camp of the prairie people. Go find him, and help him to get well. He is sad and lonely; he cries for you.'

"So I got ready and, one evening after all were asleep, I started; it was the only way. Had they known what I was about to do, my father and mother would have stopped me. I carried some food, my awl and sinews, plenty of moccasin leather. When my food was gone I snared squirrels, rabbits, dug roots. so I was never hungry. But the way was long, very, very long, and I feared the bears prowling and snuffing around in the night. They did not harm me; my dream person must have kept them from doing me wrong. The camp, my dream said, was in sight of the mountains. After many days I came to the Big River, and for many more days I followed it down, until I came in sight of the white men's houses, but I found no camp of those I sought. I turned north, and coming to the next stream, followed it up to the mountains; still I found no people. Then I went north again until I came to this little creek and now I meet you. Tell me, is my chief in your camp?"

We were, of course, obliged to tell the wanderer that her lost one was not in our camp. Weasel Tail also informed her that some North Blackfeet and some Bloods were visiting us, and advised her to accompany us and question them. She readily consented to that, and we started homeward. My friend was riding a vicious little mare which would not carry double, so I was obliged to take the woman up behind me, and we created a big sensation when we rode into camp about sundown. Weasel Tail had agreed to give her a place in his lodge, and I had hoped to drop her near it unobserved by the mistress of a certain lodge a little farther along. But no such luck. I spied Nät-ah'-ki from afar standing and gazing at us, at the handsome young woman perched behind me, her arms tightly clasped about my waist. But when I rode up to my own lodge there was no one to greet me, and for the first time I was permitted to unsaddle my animal. I went inside and sat down. Nät-ah'-ki was roasting some meat and neither spoke nor looked up. Still in silence she brought me water, soap, a towel and comb. After I had washed she set before me a bowl of soup, some meat, and then gave me a sad, reproachful look. I grinned foolishly, and, although I had been guilty of no wrong, somehow I could not return her gaze and quickly busied myself with my food. She fled to the other side of the lodge, covered her head with her shawl and began to cry. I nervously ate a little and then went out and over to Weasel Tail's.

"Send your mother over to my lodge," I said, "and have her tell Nät-ah'-ki all about it."

"Ah ha!" he laughed, "the little one is jealous? Well, we'll soon fix it," and he bade his mother go over.

An hour or two later, when I went home, Nät-ah'-ki was all smiles and welcomed me joyously, insisted that I should have another supper, and gave me a pair of gorgeous moccasins which she had been surreptitiously making for my adornment.

"Oh, that poor Snake woman," she said just before we fell asleep, "how I pity her. Tomorrow I shall make her a present of a horse."

Nät-ah'-ki was proud of her little band of horses, some of which had sprung from mares given her by relatives at various times. She loved to talk about them, to describe the color, age, and peculiarities of each one. A Blackfoot who was horseless was an object of reproach and pity. Horses were the tribal wealth, and one who owned a large herd of them held a position only to be compared to that of our millionaires. There were individuals who owned from one hundred to three and four hundred. He who could count his horses by the hundred, had gained them by many a long raid against bordering tribes, by stealing into their camps at night, by hand to hand conflict with them on many a field. No wonder he was proud of them, and of himself, and that the people honored him.

Nät-ah'-ki's band was herded by her uncle, Fish Robe, who himself had a large herd. When they were driven in, the morning after our discovery of the Snake woman, she selected a fat, potbellied roan, begged a woman's saddle from an aunt, placed it in position and led the animal over to Weasel Tail's lodge. She handed the end of the lariat to the Snake woman; at first the stranger did not comprehend her meaning; but when Nät-ah'-ki signed that the horse was to be hers, was a gift, her joy was pleasant to witness. The two women became great friends,

and she lived a part of the time with us. "I am resting," she said, "and questioning arriving visitors from other tribes. If I do not soon hear of my chief, I shall again set forth in quest of him."

One day when she and Nät-ah'-ki were gathering wood, a party of Bloods passed by on their way to our camp, and she ran after them as fast as she could, Nät-ah'-ki following and wondering if the poor woman had lost her wits. The visitors dismounted and entered our chief's lodge. The Snake woman, excited, trembling, pointed at one of the horses they rode, a black and white pinto, and signed: "I know it; my chief's horse. Ask the man where he got it."

Nät-ah'-ki went inside and made known the request to one of the women of the lodge, and the latter, as soon as there was a break in the conversation, repeated it to Big Lake. All heard her, of course, and one of the visitors spoke up: "The pinto is mine," he said, "my taking."

"Bring the woman in!" Big Lake ordered, and he told his guests about our finding her alone on the plain, about her dream and her quest.

She came inside all eagerness, the inbred diffidence of a woman facing a number of chiefs forgotten. "Who, who," she quickly signed, "is the rider of the pinto horse?"

"I am," the Blood signed. "What about it?"

"It is my horse—my man's horse, the one he rode away one morning three moons ago. And what of my man? Did you see him? How came you by his horse?"

The Blood hesitated for a moment, and then replied: "We went to war. Away south at daylight one morning, a man riding the pinto horse surprised us, and I killed him. I took the animal for my own."

As he gestured his answer, the woman suddenly noticed a bear's claw necklace he wore, and pointing to it, she gave a fearful, heartbroken, gasping sob, and fled from the lodge. She went crying through the camp, and at the edge of the timber sat down, covered her head with her robe, and began to wail for the one who was dead.

The Snake woman continued to mourn, passing the greater part of the time up on the hill, or at the edge of the timber, wailing. She cut off her hair, scarified her ankles, ate little, grew thin and listless; and finally a day came when she remained on her couch instead of arising with the others in Weasel Tail's lodge. "I am to die," she signed, "and I am glad. I did not understand my dream. I thought that I was told to seek my chief in the flesh. Instead, it was meant that my shadow should look for his shadow. I see it plainly now, and in a few nights I start. I know that I shall find him."

And start she did. She died on the fourth day of her illness, and the women buried her decently, respectfully, in a nearby tree.

CHAPTER 12

I Return to My People

THAT was a good summer. No war parties attacked us, and the young men who went out to war upon other tribes returned spoil-laden, without loss. Only one thing troubled me—the insistent letters from home, commanding me to return. They were several months old when I got them, as were my New York *Tribunes* and other papers. I ceased reading any more than the headlines; they had no interest to me, but I could not help worrying about the letters. There were grave reasons why I should heed them, should go home on or before the date that I became of age. Many an unpleasant half hour I passed after breaking their seals, and then, consigning them to the flames of the lodge fire, I would go out with Nät-ah'-ki for a ride, or to some gathering. Nät-ah'-ki spread out my letters and tried to learn what they told, although, of course, she knew not even a letter of the alphabet. She early came to know my mother's handwriting, and when I received letters from others written in characteristically feminine style, she would watch me closely as I read them and then question me as to the writers. "Oh," I would carelessly answer, "they are from relatives, women of our house, just telling me the news and asking if I am well and happy."

And then she would shake her head doubtfully, and exclaim: "Oh, yes, relatives! Tell me truly how many sweethearts you have in the land you came from!"

Then I would truthfully answer, swearing by the Sun, calling upon him to bear witness that I had but the one sweetheart, she there present, and she would be content—until I received another bundle of letters. As the summer wore on these letters became more frequent, and I realized with increasing regret that my days of happy wandering were about over, that I must go home and begin the career which was expected of me.

We left the Marias not long after the death of the Snake woman, moved south and camped on the Teton River, only three miles north of Fort Benton. Every day or so I used to ride in there, often accompanied by Nät-ah'-ki, whose desire for various bright prints, ribbons, shawls, and beads was insatiable. There we found Berry and his good wife, his mother, and the Crow woman, the two latter recently returned from a sojourn with the Mandans. And there one day came Sorrel Horse and his outfit. He and Berry were making preparations for the winter trade. I was beginning to feel pretty blue. I showed them my letters, told them what was expected of me, and declared that I must return East. They both laughed long, loudly, uproariously, and slapped each other on the back, and I gazed solemnly, reproachfully at them. I could not see that I had said anything funny.

"He's goin' home," said Sorrel Horse, "and he's goin' to be a good, quiet little boy ever after."

"And go to church," said Berry.

"And walk the straight and narrer path, world without end, and so forth," Sorrel Horse concluded.

"Well, you see how it is," I said. "I've got to go—much as I would like to remain here with you; I simply must go."

"Yes," Berry acquiesced; "you have to go all right—but you'll come back, and sooner than you think. These plains and mountains, the free life you have, and they'll never let go. I've been back there myself; went to school there, and all the time old Montana kept calling me, and I never felt right until I saw the sun shining on her bare plains once more and the Rockies looming up sharp and clear in the distance."

"And then," Sorrel Horse put in, speaking Blackfoot, which was as easy to him as English, "and then, what about Nät-ah'-ki? Can you forget her, do you think?"

He had, indeed, touched the sore spot. That was what was worrying me. I couldn't answer. We were sitting in a corner of Keno Bill's place. I jumped up from my chair, hurried out, and mounting my horse, rode swiftly over the hill to camp.

We ate our evening meal: dried meat and back fat (o-sak' i), stewed dried apples and yeast powder bread. In due time I went to bed, and for hours I rolled and tossed uneasily on my couch. "Nät-ah'-ki," I finally said, "I want to tell you something: I must go away for a time; my people call me."

"That is not news to me. I have long known that you would go."

"How did you know?" I asked. "I told no one."

"Have I not seen you read the little writings? Have I not watched your face? I know that you are going to leave me. You are no different from other white men. They marry for but a day."

She began to cry; not loud, just low, despairing, heartbroken sobs. I did hate myself, but I had opened the subject. I felt that I must carry it through, and I began to lie to her, hating myself more and more every moment. I told her that I was now twenty-one, at which time a white youth becomes a man. That there were papers about the property which my father had left, that I must go home to sign. "But," I said, and I called on the Sun to witness my words, "I will return; I will come back in a few moons, and we will once more be happy. While I am away Berry will look out for you and your good mother. You shall want for nothing."

And thus, explaining, lying, I drove away her fear and sorrow, and she fell peacefully asleep. But there was no sleep for me. In the morning I again rode in to the Fort and talked long with Berry. He agreed to look after the girl and her mother and keep them supplied with all necessary food and clothing,

until such a time, I explained, "as Nät-ah'-ki will forget me
and become some other man's woman." I nearly choked when
I said it.

Berry laughed quietly. "She will never be another man's
woman," he said. "You will be only too glad to return. I shall
see you again inside of six months."

The last steamboat of the season was discharging freight at
the levee, and was to leave for St. Louis in the morning. I went
back to camp and prepared to leave on it. There was not much
to do, merely to pack up a few native things I wished to take
home. Nät-ah'-ki rode back with me, and we passed the night
with Berry and his family. It was not a festive time to me.
Berry's mother and the faithful old Crow woman both lectured
me long and earnestly on the duty of man to woman, on faith-
fulness—and what they said hurt, for I was about to do that
which they so strongly condemned.

And so, in the morning, Nät-ah'-ki and I parted, and I shook
hands with everyone and went on board. The boat swung out
into the stream, turned around, and we went flying down the
swift current, over the Shonkin Bar and around the bend. The
old Fort, the happy days of the past year were now but a memory.

There were a number of passengers aboard, mostly miners
from Helena and Virginia City, returning to the States with
more or less dust.

They gambled, and drank, and in an effort to get rid of my
thoughts, I joined them. I remember that I lost three hundred
dollars at one sitting, and that the bad liquor made me very
ill.

We tied up to the shore each night; there were constant head
winds after we entered Dakota, and when early in October we
arrived at Council Bluffs, I was glad to leave the boat and
board the Union Pacific. In due time I arrived in the little New
England town where my home was.

I saw the place and the people with new eyes; I cared for
neither of them any more. It was a pretty place, but it was all

fenced up, and for a year I had lived where fences were unknown. The people were good people, but their ways were as
prim and conventional as were the hideous fences which
marked the bounds of their farms. And this is the way most
of them greeted me: "Ah! my boy, so you've come home, have
you? It's a wonder you wasn't scalped. Those Indians are terrible people, so I've heard. Well, you've had your fling; I suppose
you'll steady down now and go into business."

To only two men in the whole place could I tell anything of
what I had seen or done, for they were the only ones who could
understand. One was a painter, ostracized by all good people
because he never went to church and occasionally entered a
saloon in broad daylight. The other was a grocer. Both of them
were fox and partridge hunters, and loved the ways of the wild.
Night after night I sat with them by the grocery stove and
talked of the great plains and the mountains, of the game and
the red people. And in their excitement, as their minds pictured
that wonderful land and its freedom, they got up and paced the
floor, and sighed and rubbed their hands. They wanted to see
it all, to experience it all as I had, but they were "bound to the
wheel." It was impossible for them to leave home and wife and
children. I felt sorry for them.

But even to them I said nothing about another tie which
bound me to that land. There was not a moment of my waking
hours when I did not think of Nät-ah'-ki and the wrong I had
done her.

The days passed for me in deadly monotony, and I was in
constant strife with my relatives. Not with my mother, but
there were uncles and aunts, and others, old friends of my long
dead father, who tried to advise me, and shape my future. And
from the start we were antagonistic. They brought me to task
for refusing to attend church, for drinking a harmless glass of
beer with some trapper or guide from the North Woods.

There came a night when all the well-meaning ones gathered at our home. They had decided that I should buy out a
retiring merchant, who, in the course of forty or fifty years,
had acquired a modest competency. That was the last straw.

I tried to tell them what I thought of the narrow life they led; but words failed me, and, seizing my hat, I fled from the house.

It was past midnight when I returned, but my mother was waiting for me. We sat down by the fire and talked the matter out. I reminded her that from earliest youth I had preferred the forests and streams, rifle and rod, to the so-called attractions of society, and that I could not bear to live in a town or city, nor undertake a civilized occupation which would keep me confined in a store or office. And she, wise woman, agreed that as my heart was not in it, it would be useless to attempt anything of the kind. Since I had come to love the plains and mountains so well, it was best that I should return to them.

I said nothing about Nät-ah'-ki. For the first time in weeks I went to bed with a light heart.

Two days later I boarded a train, and in due time arriving in St. Louis, put up with Ben Stickney of the Planters' Hotel. There I felt in touch with things once more. I met men from Texas and Arizona, from Wyoming and Montana, and we talked of the fenceless land, of the Indians and the buffalo trade, of cattle and miners, and various adventures we had experienced. When we saw the town in true Western style, the police kindly looked the other way when our sombreroed crowd tramped by, singing at the top of our voices.

I bought another trunk, and picked up various washable things of quaint and pretty pattern, strings of beads, a pair of serpent bracelets, a gold necklace, and other articles. At last the trunk was so full that I could barely lock it, and then, gathering up my things, I boarded a train for Corinne, Wyoming. From there by stage to Helena, and on to Fort Benton.

Berry was down at the mouth of the Marias, a trader told me, with the Piegans, but his mother and the Crow woman were living in the little cabin above, and with a wink, he added that he believed a young woman was with them.

It was very early in the morning. I hurried out and up the dusty trail. A faint smoke was beginning to arise from the chimney of the little cabin. I pushed open the door and entered.

Nät-ah'-ki was kneeling before the fireplace blowing the re-
luctant flame. "Ah," she cried, springing up and running to
me, "he has come! My man has come!" She threw her arms
around my neck and kissed me, and in another instant she was
in the next room crying out: "Awake, arise; my man has returned!"

Berry's mother and the Crow woman hurried out and also
embraced and kissed me, and we all tried to talk at once, Nät-
ah'-ki hanging to my arm and gazing at me with brimming
eyes. "Ah," she said, over and over, "they kept telling me that
you would not come back, but I knew that they were wrong.
I knew that you would not forget me."

Truly, I had returned to my own. Come what might, I vowed
never to even think of leaving my woman again, and I kept
my word.

Nät-ah'-ki and I gave up attempting to eat, and she recounted all that had happened during my absence. Then she
questioned me: What had I been doing all this time? What had
I seen? Was my good mother well? I had nothing to relate. I
wanted to hear her talk, to watch her happiness, and in that
I was happy too. In due time my trunks were brought over, and
handing her the key of one, I said that it and its contents were
all hers. With exclamations of surprise and admiration she
unwrapped and unfolded the various things and spread them
out on table and couch and chairs. She threw the necklace on
over her head, clasped on the bracelets, ran over and gave me
a silent kiss, and then laid them away. "They are too nice, too
good," she said. "I am not handsome enough to wear them."

Then she came back and whispered: "But all these are too
many for me. May I give some of them to my grandmothers?"—
meaning Mrs. Berry and the Crow woman.

In the lot there were several quiet dress patterns, a couple
of shawls, which I had intended for them, and I said that they
would be appropriate gifts. How happy she was as she picked
them up and presented them to the friends.

After a while I strolled out and down to Keno Bill's place.
It was December, but the sun shone warm, a gentle chinook

was blowing. I thought of the far New England village shrouded in three feet of snow, and shivered.

I found the usual crowd in Keno's place. Judge D., a brilliant lawyer and ex-commander in the Fenian war, was playing the marshal a game of Seven-up for the drinks. Some bull-whackers and mule-skinners were bucking faro. A couple of buckskin-clad, kit-fox-capped, moccasined trappers were arguing on the best way to set a beaver trap in an ice-covered dam. They were all glad to see me, and I was promptly escorted to the bar. Several asked casually, what was new in the States? Not that they cared; they spoke of them as of some far-off and foreign country.

"Hm!" said Judge D., "you didn't remain there long, did you, my boy?"

"No," I replied, "I didn't; Montana is good enough for me."

"Montana!" cried the judge, lifting his glass. "Here's to her and her sun-kissed plains. Here's to those of us whom kind fortune has given a life within her bounds. Of all men, we are most favored of the gods."

We all cheered the toast—and drank.

By 4 o'clock in the afternoon things were pretty lively. I left the crowd and went home. The buffalo robe couch and a pipe, the open fire and Nät-ah'-ki's cheerful presence, were more to my liking.

CHAPTER 13

The Story of Rising Wolf

WHEN Berry and Sorrel Horse returned to the mouth of the Marias, Nät-ah'-ki and I, of course, went with them. Word of our coming had preceded us, and when we arrived in the great camp at dusk there we found our lodge set up between those of Talks-with-the-buffalo and Weasel Tail. Beside it was a pile of firewood; within a well-built fire was burning cheerfully; at the back our couch of soft robes and warm blankets was spread, guest seats with the comfortable backrests arranged, and in their proper place were our parfleches and cooking utensils, the former well filled with dried berries and choice dried meats and tongues and pemmican. All this had been done by Nät-ah'-ki's good mother, who greeted her daughter with a hearty hug and kiss and me with a shy but sincere welcome.

I had no sooner got down from the wagon and gone inside, leaving Nät-ah'-ki and her mother to bring in our possessions, than my friends began to arrive.

They told me briefly of the happenings during my absence, and then asked for the story of my trip. While Nät-ah'-ki prepared a little feast, and they smoked, I gave it to them as well as I could, giving the number of days that I had traveled on the steamboat, and then on the train, a distance in all of a hundred nights' sleep were one to travel it on horseback. I had

91

to repeat the story several times that night, once in the chief's lodge. When I had finished the old man inquired particularly about the railroad and its trains, fire-wagons—is-tsi' an'-e-kas-im—as he called them. He wanted to know if any of them were heading for this country.

"No," I replied, "none are coming this way; there is but the one, that which runs east and west far south of here, through the land of the Wolf People and the Sheep Eaters."

"Ai!" he said, thoughtfully stroking his chin, "Ai! that one many of us have seen on our raids to the south. Yes, we have seen it, the wagons, crowded with people, roaring across the plain, killing and scaring the buffalo. Some day you write to our Grandfather (the President) and tell him that we will not allow one to enter our country. Yes, tell him that I, Big Lake, send him this word: 'The white men shall neither put a fire-wagon trail across the country of my people, nor settle here and tear up the sod of our valleys in order to plant the things they feed upon.'"

I attended many a feast that night, no sooner finishing a visit at one lodge than I was invited to another one. It was late when I finally returned home and lay down to rest, the song and laughter of the great camp, the howling of the wolves and coyotes lulling me to sleep. I thought of the New England village buried in deep snow, and of its dreary monotony. "Thrice blest am I by propitious gods," I murmured.

Nät-ah'-ki nudged me. "You talk in your sleep," she said.

"I was not asleep; I was thinking aloud."

"And what thought you?"

"The gods pity me," I replied. "They have been kind to me and given me much happiness."

"Ai!" she acquiesced; "they are good; we could ask of them nothing that they have not given us. Tomorrow we will sacrifice to them."

I fell asleep, determined that, save perhaps for an occasional visit, the East should know me no more.

The following day the chiefs and leading men decided that we should move out to the foot of the Bear's Paw Mountains.

We went across the wide, brown and buffalo-covered plain, encamping on a little stream running down from a pine-clad coulée, remaining there for several days. There were vast numbers of elk and deer and big-horn here, and in our morning's hunt Wolverine and I killed four fat ewes, choosing the females instead of the rams, as the rutting season of the sheep was nearly over.

When I returned to camp I found Nät-ah'-ki busily chipping the hide of a cow buffalo I had killed. She had laced it to a frame of four lodge poles and frozen it, in which condition the surplus thickness of the hide was most easily removed with the short elk-horn, steel-tipped hoe used for the purpose. But even then it was exceedingly hard, back-breaking labor, and I said I would be pleased if she would cease doing that kind of work. I had said something about it on a previous occasion, and this time, perhaps, I spoke a trifle too peremptorily. She turned away from me, but not before I saw the tears begin to roll down her cheeks.

"What have I done?" I asked. "I did not mean to make you cry."

"Am I to do nothing?" she queried, "but sit in the lodge in idleness? You hunt and provide the meat; you buy from the traders the foods we eat. You buy my clothes and everything else I wear and use. I also want to do something toward our support."

"But you do. You cook and wash the dishes, you even provide the firewood. You make my moccasins and warm mittens; you wash my clothes; when we travel it is you who take down and set up the lodge, who pack and unpack the horses."

"Yet am I idle most of the time," she said brokenly, "and the women jest and laugh at me, and call me too proud and too lazy to work!"

Thereupon I kissed her and told her to tan as many robes as she wanted to, taking care not to work too hard nor too long at a time. And immediately she was all smiles and danced out of the lodge; presently I heard the monotonous chuck, chuck of the hoe tip against the stiff hide.

One night a dimly luminous ring was seen around the moon, and the next morning a brighter ring encircled the sun, while on either side of it was a large sun-dog. The rings portended the arrival of a furious storm at no distant date; the rainbow-hued sun-dogs gave certain warning that the enemy, perhaps a large war party, was approaching our camp. This was a bad combination, and a council was called to consider it. The tribe was not afraid to meet any enemy that might do battle with them, but it was certain that in the night of a severe storm a party could approach unseen and unheard, steal many horses, and that the driving, drifting snow would effectually blot out their trail, so that they could not be followed and overtaken. It was decided to break camp at once and move to the mouth of Creek-in-the-middle, on the Missouri. If much snow fell and severe, cold weather set in, there would be better shelter in the deep valley of the river; the horses could be fed the rich bark of the cottonwood and kept in prime condition; by moving camp the certainly approaching enemy would probably never run across our trail, especially if the promised storm came soon. By ten o'clock the last lodge was down and packed, and we strung out east by south for our destination. At noon snow began to fall. We camped that night on Creek-in-the-middle, so named because it has its source midway between the Bear's Paw and Little Rocky Mountains. The early voyageurs named it Cow Creek.

Snow was still lightly falling the next morning and it was much colder; nevertheless, we moved on, arriving at the river before dusk. Here we intended to remain for some time, and the hunters rode far and near on both sides of the valley and out on the plains setting deadfalls for wolves. These deadfalls were merely a few six foot to eight foot poles set up at an angle of about forty-five degrees and supported by a two-stick trigger. They were covered with several hundredweight of large stones; when the wolf seized the bait at the back end of the fall, down came the heavy roof and crushed him. Berry and Sorrel Horse did all they could to encourage the trapping of the animals, as a large demand had sprung up for their skins in the States, where they were converted into sleigh robes. Prime skins were selling in Fort Benton at from four to five dollars each.

The storm did not amount to much, and in a few days a warm chinook again set in. Nor did the expected war party appear. My friends, the traders, were doing such a good business that they were obliged to go after more goods every two or three weeks, or whenever they could join a party bound for Fort Benton.

I had heard much of a certain white man named Hugh Monroe, or, in Blackfoot, Rising Wolf—Mah-kwo-i-pwo-ahts. One afternoon I was told that he had arrived in camp with his numerous family, and a little later met him at a feast given by Big Lake. In the evening I invited him over to my lodge and had a long talk with him while we ate bread and meat and beans, and smoked numerous pipefuls of tobacco. Even in his old age, Rising Wolf was about the quickest, most active man I ever saw. He was about five feet six in height, fair-haired, blue-eyed, and his firm, square chin and rather prominent nose betokened what he was; a man of courage and determination. His father, Hugh Monroe, was a colonel in the British army, his mother a member of the La Roche, a noble family of French emigrés, bankers of Montreal, and large land owners in that vicinity. Hugh, Jr., was born on the family estate at Three Rivers, and attended the parish school just long enough to learn to read and write. All of his vacations, and many truant days from the classroom, were spent in the great forest surrounding his home.

In 1813, when fifteen years of age, he persuaded his parents to allow him to enter the service of the Hudson's Bay Company and started westward with a flotilla of their canoes that spring. His father gave him a fine English smooth-bore, his mother a pair of the famous La Roche dueling pistols and a prayer book. The family priest gave him a rosary and cross, and enjoined him to pray frequently. Traveling all summer they arrived at Lake Winnipeg in the autumn and wintered there. As soon as the ice went out in the spring the journey was continued, and one afternoon in July, Monroe beheld Mountain Fort,

a new post of the company, built on the south bank of the
Saskatchewan River, nor far from the foot of the Rockies.

Around about it were encamped thousands of the Blackfeet
waiting to trade for the goods the flotilla had brought up, and
to obtain on credit ammunition, fukes, traps, and tobacco sufficient to last them through the coming season. As yet the
company had no Blackfoot interpreter, their speech having
first to be translated into Cree, and then into English. Many
of the Blackfeet proper, the North Blackfeet, spoke good Cree;
but the more southern tribes of the confederacy, the Bloods
and Piegans, did not understand it. The factor, no doubt per-
ceiving that Monroe was a youth of more than ordinary intel-
ligence, at once detailed him to live and travel with the Piegans
and learn the language, also to see that they returned to Mountain Fort with their furs the succeeding summer. Word had
been received that, following the course of Lewis and Clark,
American traders were yearly pushing farther and farther
westward, and had even reached the mouth of the Yellowstone,
about the eastern line of the vast territory claimed by the
Blackfeet as their hunting ground. The company feared their
competition; Monroe was to do his best to prevent it.

"At last the day came for our departure," Monroe told me,
"and I set out with the chiefs and medicine men at the head
of the long procession. There were eight hundred lodges of the
Piegans there, about eight thousand people. They owned thousands of horses. It was a grand sight to see that long column
of riders, and travois, and pack animals, and loose horses troop-
ing over the plains. We traveled southward all day, and before
sundown came to the rim of a valley through which flowed a
fine cottonwood-bordered stream. We dismounted at the top of
the hill, and spread our robes, intending to sit there until the
procession passed by into the bottom and put up the lodges. A
medicine man produced a large stone pipe, filled it and attempted to light it with flint and steel and a bit of punk, but
somehow he could get no spark. I motioned him to hand it to
me, and, drawing my sun glass from my pocket I got the proper

focus and set the tobacco afire, drawing several mouthfuls of smoke through the long stem. As one man, all those sitting round about sprang to their feet and rushed toward me, shouting and gesticulating as if they had gone crazy. I also jumped up, terribly frightened, for I thought they were going to kill me; but for what I could not imagine. The pipe was wrenched out of my grasp by the chief himself, who eagerly began to smoke and pray. He had drawn but a whiff or two, however, when another seized it and from him it was taken by still another. Others turned and harangued the passing column; men and women sprang from their horses and joined the group, mothers pressing close and rubbing their babes against me, praying earnestly meanwhile. I recognized a word that I had already learned—natos'—Sun; and suddenly the meaning of the commotion became clear; they thought that I was great medicine; that I had called upon the Sun himself to light my pipe, and that he had done so. The mere act of holding my hand up above the pipe was a supplication to their god. At all events, I had suddenly become a great personage.

"When I entered Lone Walker's lodge that evening—he was the chief, and my host—I was greeted by deep growls from either side of the doorway, and was horrified to see two nearly grown grizzly bears acting as if about to spring upon me. I stopped and stood quite still, but I believe that my hair was rising. Lone Walker spoke to his pets and they immediately lay down, noses between their paws, and I passed on to the place pointed out to me, the first couch at the chief's left hand. It was some time before I became accustomed to the bears, but we finally came to a sort of understanding with one another. They ceased growling at me as I passed in and out of the lodge, but would never allow me to touch them. In the following spring they disappeared one night and were never seen again. Lone Walker went about for days hunting and calling them, but in vain. It has been said that a grizzly cannot be tamed; those two at least seemed to have a real liking for their master, who alone fed them; they were never tied up and followed the travois of his family along with the dogs when we moved camp, always sleeping where I first saw them on either side of the doorway."

Monroe often referred to that first trip with the Piegans as the happiest time of his life. Journeying by easy stages, sometimes skirting the foot of the mountains, and again traversing the broad plains forty or fifty miles to the eastward they came, at the season of falling leaves, to the Pile of Rocks River (Sun River, as the whites named it), and there they remained for three months, passing the remainder of the winter on the Yellow River (the Judith). They had crossed Lewis and Clark's trail, and here again was a vast region which no white man had ever traversed. When spring came, they went still further south, crossed the Missouri, and wandered westward to the Marias and its tributaries. It had been long since decided that they would not return to Mountain Fort until the following summer. Rifle and pistol were now useless, as the last rounds of powder and ball had been fired. But they had their bows and great sheafs of arrows.

One by one young Rising Wolf's garments were worn out and cast aside. The women of the lodge tanned skins of deer and bighorn, and from them Lone Walker himself cut and sewed shirts and leggings, which he wore in their place. It was not permitted for women to make men's clothing. Ap'-ah-ki, the shy young daughter of the chief, made his footwear—thin, parfleche-soled moccasins for summer, beautifully embroidered with colored porcupine quills; thick, soft, warm ones of buffalo robe for winter.

"I could not help but notice her," Lone Walker said, "on the first night I stayed in her father's lodge. Of good height and slender but well-formed figure, comely face and beautiful eyes, long-haired, quick and graceful in all her movements, she was indeed good to see. I fell into the habit of looking at her when I thought no one was observing me, and before long I found that it suited me better to stay in the lodge where I could at least be near her than it did to go hunting or on discovery with the men. I learned the language easily, quickly; yet I never spoke to her, nor she to me, for, as you know, the Blackfeet think it unseemly.

"One evening a man came into the lodge and began to praise a youth with whom I had often hunted; spoke of his bravery, his kindness, his wealth, and ended by saying that the young fellow presented to Lone Walker thirty horses, and wished, with Ap'-ah-ki, to set up a lodge of his own. I glanced at the girl and caught her looking at me, a look expressing at once fear, despair and something else. The chief spoke: 'Tell your friend,' he said, 'that all you have spoken of him is true; I know that he is a real man, a good, kind, brave, generous young man, yet for all that I cannot give him my daughter.'

"Again I looked at Ap'-ah-ki, and she at me. Now she was smiling, and there was happiness in her eyes. But if she smiled, I could not, for Lone Walker's words had killed any hope I might have had of getting her some day for my own. I had heard him refuse thirty head of horses. What hope had I then, who did not own even the horse I rode, I who received for my services only twenty pounds a year, from which must be deducted the articles I bought. Surely the girl was not for me.

"After that night Ap'-ah-ki no longer cast down her eyes when I caught her looking at me, but returned my gaze openly, fearlessly, lovingly. We now knew that we loved each other. One day I met her in the trail bringing home a bundle of firewood. We stopped and looked at each other in silence, and then I spoke her name. Crash went the fuel on the ground, and we embraced and kissed, regardless of those who might be looking.

"'I can stand this no longer,' I said at last. 'Come with me now to your father, and I will speak to him.'

"'Yes,' she whispered. 'Yes; let us take courage, and go to him. He has always been good to me, and perhaps he will be generous now.'

"So, forgetting the bundle of wood, we went hand in hand and stood before Lone Walker, where he sat smoking his long pipe, out on the shady side of the lodge. 'I have not thirty horses,' I said, 'nor even one, but I love your daughter, and she loves me. I ask you to give her to me.'

"The chief smiled, 'Why think you, did I refuse the thirty horses?' he asked. 'Because I wanted you for my son-in-law; wanted a white man because he is more cunning, much wiser than the Indian. We have not been blind, neither I nor my women. We have long seen that this day was coming—have waited for you to speak the word. You have spoken; there is nothing more to say except this: be good to her.'

"That very day they set up a small lodge for us and stored it with robes and parfleches of dried meat and berries, gave us one of their two brass kettles, tanned skins, pack saddles, ropes—all that a lodge should contain. And, not least, Lone Walker told me to choose thirty horses from his large herd."

The old man paused and sat silent, thinking of the old days.

"I know how you felt," I said, "for we are experiencing the same thing."

"I know it," he continued; "seeing the peace and contentment and happiness in this lodge, I could not help telling you about my own youthful days."

Monroe never revisited his home; never saw his parents after the day they parted with him at the Montreal docks. He intended to return to them for a brief visit some time, but kept deferring it, and then came letters, two years old, saying that they were both dead. Came also a letter from an attorney, saying that they had bequeathed him a considerable property, that he must go to Montreal and sign papers in order to take possession of it.

At the time the factor of Mountain Fort was going to England on leave; to him, in his simple trustfulness, Monroe gave a power of attorney in the matter. The factor never returned, and by virtue of the papers he had signed, the frontiersman lost his inheritance. But that was a matter of little moment to him then. Had he not a lodge and family, good horses and a vast domain actually teeming with game—wherein to wander—what more could one possibly want?

Leaving the Hudson's Bay Company, Monroe sometimes worked for the American Fur Company, but mostly as a free trapper wandered from the Saskatchewan to the Yellowstone, and from the Rockies to Lake Winnipeg. The headwaters of the South Saskatchewan were one of his hunting grounds. There in the early '50's he guided the noted Jesuit, Father De Smet, and at the foot of the beautiful lakes lying just south of Chief Mountain they erected a huge wooden cross, and named the two bodies of water St. Mary's Lakes. One winter after his sons, John and François, had married, they were camping there for the season, the three lodges of the family, when a large war party of Assiniboins attacked them. The daughters, Lizzie, Amelia, and Mary, had been taught to shoot, and together they made a brave resistance, driving the Indians away with the loss of five of their number, Lizzie killing one of them as he was about to let down the bars of the horse corral.

Besides other furs, beaver, fisher, martin, and wolverines, they killed more than three hundred wolves that winter. By the banks of the outlet of the lakes they built a long pen twelve by sixteen feet at the base, and sloping sharply inward and upward to a height of seven feet; the top of the pyramid was an opening about two and one-half feet wide by eight in length. Whole deer, quarters of buffalo, any kind of meat handy, was thrown into the pen, and the wolves, scenting the flesh and blood, seeing it plainly through the four to six inch spaces between the logs, would eventually climb to the top and jump down through the opening. But they could not jump out, and there morning would find them uneasily pacing around and around in utter bewilderment. Powder and balls were precious commodities in those days, so the trappers killed the wolves with bow and arrows, and opening a door at one end, they allowed the coyotes to escape. The carcasses of the slain wolves were always thrown into the river as soon as skinned, so that there should be nothing of a suspicious nature about.

Rising Wolf was always bemoaning the decadence of the Indians—the Piegans in particular. "You should have seen them in the long ago, he would say; "such a proud and brave people they were. But now, there are no longer any great chiefs, and the medicine men have lost their power."

He used often to speak of the terrible power possessed by a medicine man named Old Sun. "There was one," he would say, "who surely talked with the gods, and was given some of their mysterious power. Sometimes of a dark night, he would invite a few of us to his lodge, when all was calm and still. After all were seated his wives would bank the fire with ashes so that it was dark, and he would begin to pray. First to the Sun, chief ruler, then to Ai-so-pwom-stan, the wind-maker, then to Sis-tse-kom, the thunder, and Puh-pom', the lightning. As he prayed, entreating them to come and do his will, first the lodge ears would begin to quiver with the first breath of a coming breeze, which gradually grew stronger until the lodge bent to the blasts, and the poles strained and creaked. Then thunder began to boom, faint and far away, and lightning to dimly blaze, and they came nearer and nearer until they seemed to be just overhead; the crashes deafened us, the flashes blinded us. Then this wonderful man would pray them to go, and the wind would die down and the thunder and lightning go on rumbling and flashing into the far distance until we heard and saw them no more."

All this the old man firmly believed that he had heard and seen.

CHAPTER 14

A Friendly Visit from the Crows

IN the days of which I write the Blackfeet were not, as they are now, cursed with the different forms of tuberculosis. Yet there were, of course, occasional cases. The wife of Four Horns, a young man of the Small Robe band, had it, and was growing steadily worse. As the lodge of the young couple was quite near ours, we naturally saw much of them. Four Horns was an exceedingly tall, well-built, pleasant-featured man of twenty-eight or thirty, and his wife was also good looking, neat in person and habits, but the disease had wasted her once fine form. The man was a famous raider, a tireless hunter, and, with what he had taken from the enemy, and by careful breeding, had acquired a large band of horses. In his lodge were always bundles of fine robes and furs, ready to be bartered for anything that was needed or which took his wife's fancy. Nothing was too good for his woman; he thought the world of her, and she of him.

When the disease appeared a doctor was called in and given a fee of three horses. His medicines and prayers did no good, however, and another one was tried—fee, five horses—but with like results. In succession the doctors of the whole tribe at-

tended the patient, and now the end was near. The fine herd
of horses had shrunk to less than a dozen head. Robes, furs,
costly blankets, and finery had also been given to the doctors.
Late one evening a messenger hurriedly entered our lodge:
"You are called," he said, "by Four Horns; he bids you, both of
you, make haste."

We found the poor woman gasping for breath. Four Horns
was sitting on the couch beside her, his face buried in his hands.
An old woman, robe thrown over her head, was feeding the
fire. I poured out a large drink of whisky, added some sugar
and hot water to it, and Nät-ah'-ki gave it to the sufferer. It
revived her; she soon breathed more easily, and then said to
me, speaking very slowly and interruptedly: "Never in all my
life have I done a wrong thing. I have never lied, nor stolen,
nor done that which brings shame upon a woman's parents and
upon her. Yet our gods have forsaken me and I am near to
death. You have gods as well as we. I have heard of them. The
Maker, His Son, the Mother of the Son. Pray to them, I beg
you; perhaps they will take pity and make me well."

I cannot explain, I fear, how I felt upon hearing that simple
request. I wished that I could grant it, and knew that I could
not. How was it possible for one to pray who had no faith? I
cast about in my mind for some excuse; for something to say,
for some way to explain my inability to do it. I looked up and
found Nät-ah'-ki earnestly, expectantly gazing at me. We had
talked about religion, the white man's religion, several times,
and she knew that I had no faith in it. Nevertheless, I could
see that she expected me to do what the dying woman had
requested. I made the sign of negation. She moved at once to
the side of the sufferer and said: "I will pray to those gods for
you. Long ago, when I was a little girl, a Blackrobe and my
uncle taught me the way." She began: "Ap'-ai-stu-to-ki, kin'-
ah-an-on, etc." 'Twas the Lord's prayer! Some zealous Jesuit,
perhaps Father De Smet himself, had translated it into Blackfoot, and good Blackfoot, too.

But even as the prayer ended, a dark stream flowed from
the woman's mouth, the last and fatal hemorrhage. "That

which kills you," cried Four Horns, "shall kill me. I follow you soon to the Sandhills." And bending over he drank of the blood flowing from his loved one's lips. With one last effort she clasped her thin arms around his neck, and died. It was a dreadful scene.

"Come," I said presently, gently lifting him. "Come with me to my lodge; the women now have their work to do."

With one last, long look, he arose and followed me. I gave him the guest couch, and handed him a cupful of whisky which he quickly swallowed. After a time I gave him another cupful. Worn out with long watching, overcome by the strong liquor, he lay down and I covered him with a robe. He slept soundly until after noon the next day; by that time Nät-ah'-ki and others had bound the body in robes and blankets and lashed it in a tree somewhere down the river. I don't know whether Four Horns had long before contracted the disease, or if he was infected at his wife's death bed. He died of the same dread scourge six weeks later. If there is a Sandhills, let us hope that his shadow found hers.

In February we were visited by a deputation from the Crows, who were wintering on Tongue River, away to the south of us. They came with tobacco and other presents from their chief to ours, and the message that their people offered to make a lasting treaty of peace with the Piegans.

Their leader was Rock Eater, half Crow and half Blackfoot. His mother had been captured by the former tribe when a young girl, and in due time became the wife of her captor's son. Rock Eater, of course, spoke both languages perfectly. The envoys were well received, and became guests of the more prominent men. Their proposition was one which required mature deliberation, and while the chiefs and head warriors were discussing it, they were feasted and given the best of everything in the camp. Rock Eater himself became my guest, and many an interesting talk I had with him by the evening fire.

"Is your mother happy with the Crows?" I asked him one night. "And how do you yourself feel—that you are Piegan, or Crow, or both?"

"It is this way," he replied. "My mother loves my father, and I love him, for he has always been kind to us. Generally, we are quite happy; but there are times, when a party returns with Piegan scalps, or horses taken from them, boasting loudly of their victory, calling the Piegans cowardly dogs. Then we feel very sad. And often the proud young Crows have made fun of me, and joked about me, calling me bad names. Long ago my mother began to urge my father to talk with the chiefs and urge them to make peace with her people. I have also long been saying what I could to help the plan. But always one chief would arise and say, 'The Piegans killed my son; I want revenge, not peace.' Others would speak, crying out that they had lost a brother, or father, or uncle, or nephew in war with the Piegans, and that they could not think of making peace. Not long ago my father again called a council to consider this question, and as ever, he was opposed by many of the leading men. The last speaker said this to him: 'We are tired of being asked to talk about making peace with the Piegans. If you are so anxious to be friendly with them, why not go and live with them; become a Piegan yourself.'

"'So I will,' cried my father in anger. 'So I will. I will become a Piegan, and fight with them against all their enemies.' And so saying, he arose and went home, I following him.

"Now, my father is a chief himself; a fearless man in war, so kindly and generous that he is loved by all but a few who are jealous of his position. When it was learned what he said in the council, the people came to him and begged him to take back his words; also they went to the other chiefs and insisted that peace should be declared, provided the Piegans would agree to it. 'We have had enough of this war,' they said. 'See the widows and orphans it has made. We have our own great country covered with buffalo; the Piegans have theirs; the two tribes can live without killing one another.' So, after all, my father had his way, and we were sent to you. I hope we will carry Piegan tobacco back with us."

Rock Eater was called to a feast, and soon after Rising Wolf came in to smoke a pipe with me. I asked him to tell me something about the wars between the two tribes.

"The Blackfeet are a northern people," he began, "who once lived in the Slave Lake country. The Crees named those lakes after them, because they made slaves of the enemies they captured. Gradually they began to journey southward and came to these great plains abounding in game, where the winters are mild. There they found different tribes—Crows, Assiniboins, Shoshones, and various mountain tribes, the Kutenais, Pend d'Oreilles, and Stonies—and drove all before them, taking possession of their country. There were times of peace between them and these tribes, but mostly they waged war upon them.

"In 1832 the Blackfeet made a treaty of peace with the Crows, at Fort Union, which lasted only two years. Again, in 1855, at the mouth of the Judith River, at what is known as the Stevens treaty between the United States and various tribes, the Blackfeet, Crows, Gros Ventres, Pend d'Oreilles, the Kutenais, Nez Percés and others agreed to cease warring against one another, and intruding upon each other's hunting grounds. The Musselshell River was designated as the boundary separating Blackfeet from Crow territory. In the summer of 1857 the Crows broke this agreement by raiding a camp of the Bloods, killing two men and running off a large number of horses. That reopened the old feud, the three Blackfeet tribes, Bloods, Piegans and Blackfeet proper, making common cause against the enemy. In the fall of 1858 I joined the Piegans with my family at Fort Benton, and we went south of the Missouri to winter.

"Our column was loosely scattered along four or five miles of the trail that day, and most of the hunters were behind, away to the east and west, skinning buffalo and other game they had killed; ahead of us a mile or so rode our scouts, some thirty or forty men. The Scouts gave no sign that they had seen anything to make them suspicious. The old people dozed in their saddles; young men here and there were singing; the mother crooned to the babe at her breast; all were happy.

"The scouts passed out of view down the south slope of the gap, and the head of our column was nearing the summit, when out from a large pine grove on our right dashed at least two hundred mounted Crows, and fell upon us. Back turned the people, the women and old men madly urging their horses, scattering travois and lodge poles along the way, shrieking for help, calling on the gods to preserve them. Such fighting men as there were along this part of the line did their utmost to check the rush of the Crows, to cover the retreat of the weak and defenseless. Hearing shots and shouts, back came the scouts, and from the rear came charging more men to the front. But in spite of stubborn resistance the Crows swept all before them for a distance of at least two miles, strewing the trail with our dead and dying people—men, women, children, even babies.

"They took not one captive, but shot and struck, and lanced to kill, scalping many of their victims. But at last the Piegans bunched up in some sort of order, and the Crows drew off and rode away to the south, singing their songs of victory, taunting us by waving in triumph the scalps they had taken. So badly had our people been stampeded, so stunned were they by the calamity that they simply stood and stared at the retreating enemy, instead of following them.

"Right there in the gap the lodges were pitched, and search for the dead and missing begun. For weeks and months, when evening came, the wailing of the mourners, sitting out in the darkness just beyond the circle of the lodges, was pitiful to hear. I happened to be with the scouts that day, and when we charged back did my best with them to check the Crows. But they had so demoralized the people that we were powerless until our men in the rear came up. More than half the scouts were killed. I got an arrow in the left thigh. In all, one hundred and thirteen Piegans were killed, while we shot down but seven of the enemy.

"After this happened, you may be sure that most of the war parties leaving the Piegan camp headed for the Crow country, and from the north came parties of their brothers, the Blackfeet and Bloods, to harass the common enemy. In the course of two or three years they killed enough members of the Crow tribe, and drove off sufficient numbers of their horse herds, to more than offset their own losses in the massacre and in later fights—for, of course, our war parties were not always victorious.

"In the spring of 1867 the Gros Ventres—then at war with the Blackfeet tribes—concluded a treaty with the Crows, and there was a great gathering of them all on lower Milk River, to celebrate the event. A party of young Gros Ventres returning from a raid against the Crees brought word that they had seen the Piegan camp in the Divided—or Cypress—Hills. This was great news. The Crows had a long score to settle with their oldtime enemy. So also felt the Gros Ventres. Although they had for a very long time been under the protection of the Blackfeet, who fought their battles for them, and protected them from their bitter foes, the Assiniboins and Yanktonais, they had no gratitude in their make-up, and had quarreled with their benefactors over a trivial cause. And now for revenge! So sure were they of success, that they had their women accompany them to sort out and care for the prospective plunder.

"From a distant butte the war party had seen the Piegan camp, but had not discovered that just over a hill to the west of it, not half a mile further, the Bloods were encamped in force, some five thousand of them, or in all about one thousand fighting men. So one morning the Crows and Gros Ventres came trailing leisurely over the plain toward the Piegan camp; the plumes of their war bonnets and the eagle feather fringe of their shields fluttering gaily in the wind. And with them came their women, already rejoicing over the vast store of plunder they were going to possess. An early hunter from the Piegan camp, going with his woman after some meat he had killed the previous day, discovered the enemy and hurried back to give the alarm, sending one of his women on to call out the Bloods. There was a great rush for horses, for weapons. And thus when the attacking party came tearing over the little rise of ground just east of the camp they were met by such an overwhelming force of determined men that they turned and fled, firing but few shots. Better mounted than their women, they left these defenseless ones to our mercy, seeking only to escape themselves.

"From the point of meeting a slaughter began. Big Lake, Little Dog, Three Suns, and other chiefs kept shouting to their men to spare the women, but a few were killed before they could make their commands known. The fleeing men were overtaken and shot, or brained with war clubs. For miles the trail was strewn with the dead and dying, through which fled their women, shrieking with terror—the women they had brought to care for their plunder. 'Let them go!' cried Big Lake, laughing. 'Let them go! We will do as did Old Man with the rabbits, leave a few to breed, so that their kind may not become wholly extinct.'

"A count was made of the dead. Only five of the Blackfeet had lost their lives, and a few been wounded. But along the trail over which they had so confidently marched that morning three hundred and sixty Crows and Gros Ventres lay dead. Many of them were never touched, for the victors had become tired of cutting and scalping. Their arms were taken, however, and in many cases their war costumes and ornaments, and then the two camps moved westward a way, leaving the battlefield to the wolf and coyote.

"As you know, the Gros Ventres asked for peace, and are again under the protection of our people. And now come these messengers from the Crows. Well, we will see what we will see." And bidding us sleep well, Rising Wolf—I never could call him Monroe—went home.

When Berry was in camp, or anywhere within a reasonable distance of it, the Piegans did no business without consulting him, and they always took his advice. Their chiefs deferred to him, relied upon him, and he never failed to advise that which was for their best interests. So now he was called to attend the council to consider the Crow proposal, and I went, too, under his wing. Big Lake's lodge was well filled with the chiefs and leading men of the tribe, including the younger heads of the different bands of the All Friends Society, who acted as camp police. Among them I noticed my enemy, Little Deer, who scowled at me when I entered. He was beginning to get on my nerves. To tell the truth, I impatiently looked forward to the day when we would have it out, being possessed of a sort of unreasoning belief that I was fated some day to send his shadow to the Sandhills.

Big Lake filled his big stone pipe, a medicine man lighted it, made a short prayer, and then it was passed back and forth around the circle. Three Suns opened the subject for consideration by saying that he and his band, the Lone Eaters, favored a peace treaty with their old enemy. He had no sooner finished than Little Deer began an impassioned harangue. He should have been one of the last to speak, older men and those of higher position having precedence over the younger; but he thrust himself forward. Nevertheless, he was listened to in silence.

Little Deer said that he represented the Raven Carrier band of the great society, and that they wanted no peace with the Crows. Who were the Crows but murderers of their fathers and brothers; stealers of their herds? As soon as green grass came, he concluded, he and his friends would start on a raid against the people of the Elk River (Yellowstone), and that raid would be repeated again and again while summer lasted.

One after another each one had his say, many declaring for a peace treaty, a few—generally the younger men—voicing Little Deer's sentiments. I remember especially the speech of an ancient, blind, white-haired medicine man.

"Oh, my children!" he began, "when I was young like some of you here, I was happiest when raiding the enemy, killing them, driving off their horses. I became rich. My women bore me four fine sons; my lodge was always filled with good food, fine furs. My boys grew up, strong, active, good raiders and good shots. 'You grow old; sit you here by the lodge fire and smoke and dream, and we will provide for you,' they told me. I was happy, grateful. I looked forward to many pleasant winters as I aged. Hai-ya! One after another my sons went forth

to war, and one after another they failed to return. Two of my
women were also killed by the enemy; another died, and she
who remains is old and feeble. I am blind and helpless; we are
both dependent on our friends for what we eat and wear, and
for a place by the lodge fire. This is truly a most unhappy
condition. But if there had been no war—ai! If there had been
no war, then this day I would be in my own lodge with my
children and grandchildren, and my women, all of us happy
and content. You who have talked against peace, think hard
and take back your words. What war has done to me, it surely
will do to some of you."

When the old man finished, nearly every one in the lodge
cried "Ah!" "Ah!" in approval of his speech. Big Lake then
spoke a few words: "I was going to make a talk for peace," he
said, "but our blind friend has spoken better than I could; his
words are my words. Let us hear from our friend the trader
chief."

"I say with you," Berry agreed, "that the old man's talk is
my talk. Better the camp of peace and plenty than the mourn-
ing of widows and orphans out in the darkness beyond the fires.
Let us make peace."

"It shall be peace!" said Big Lake. "Only six of you here have
talked against it, and you are far outnumbered. I shall tell the
Crow messengers that we will meet their people at Fort Benton,
and there make friends. I have said. Go you forth."

Back at my lodge I found Rock Eater talking with Nät-ah´-
ki. I saw at once that she was excited about something, and as
soon as I had told our friend the decision of the council, she
began: "See what we have discovered. His mother—" pointing
at Rock Eater—"is my mother's cousin, my relative; he is my
relative. How queer it is; he came into our lodge a stranger,
and we discover that he is of our blood, our very own family!
And you say that we are to meet the Crows when the berries
ripen. Oh, I am glad; glad! How pleased my mother will be to
see her whom we thought was dead. Oh, we will be good to her.
We will make her forget all that she has suffered."

I reached over and shook hands with Rock Eater. "Friend and relative," I said, "I am glad to hear this news."

And I was glad. I had taken a strong liking to the young man, who in his plain and simple way had told us of his sufferings and humiliations among a partly alien—one may say wholly alien—people, for, after all, the mother's kin, and not the father's are almost invariably the chosen kin of the offspring of a marriage between members of different tribes or nations.

The All Friends Society gave a dance in honor of the visitors, a Parted Hair, or Sioux dance, which was a grand and spectacular performance. Not to be outdone, the Crows decided to give one of their own peculiar dances, one called the Dog Feast dance. But at the very mention of it, the Piegans suddenly lost all interest. Not that they didn't want to see the dance; they were anxious to see it.

The hitch was about the dog. To them it was a sacred animal, never to be killed, nor worse still, to be used as an article of food. Dreading the wrath of the gods, none of them even dared to give the visitors one, knowing that it would be killed and eaten. I solved the problem by buying one from an old woman, pretending that I wanted it for a watch dog, and then giving it to the Crows. It was a large, fat, ancient dog, nearly toothless, purblind and furred like a wolf. The Crows led it down into the timber by the river, and when next I saw it, it was hanging in a tree, dressed and scraped, its skin as white and shiny as that of a newly butchered pig.

The next day they wanted a kettle in which to stew the dog, and no one dared loan one for such a purpose. Again I went to the rescue, "borrowed" two empty five-gallon alcohol cans from Berry and donated them. In these the dog meat was cooked to perfection.

These Crows had about the handsomest war costumes I ever saw. Every eagle-tail feather of their headdresses was perfect, and the hanging part of them swept the ground at their heels. Their shirts and leggings were elegantly fringed with weasel skins, scalp locks and buckskin, and embroidered, as were their belts and moccasins, with complex designs in perfectly laid porcupine quills of gorgeous colors. The steaming cans of dog meat were carried to a level, open place between the camp and the river, and placed by a freshly built fire. Two of the Crows began to beat a drum, and the dance began, an immense crowd having gathered around in a great circle to see it. No one cared to go near the cans of forbidden food. Forth and back they danced, now to the right, again to the left, every little while circling completely around the fire and the cans, arms and hands extended, as if blessing the food.

The performance lasted about an hour, and then the party removed the cans from the fire and prepared to feast. In less than two minutes the last Piegan had left the vicinity, some of the women badly nauseated at the thought of eating such proscribed food.

After remaining with us a couple of days longer, the Crows prepared to depart, and many a present was given them for themselves and for their chief. They carried about ten pounds of tobacco as a token that the Piegans accepted their overtures of peace, also a handsome black stone pipe, a present from Big Lake to their head chief. Then they were given a number of horses, fine blankets, parfleches of choice dried meat and skins of pemmican. Nät-ah'-ki had her little herd run in.

"My horses are your horses," she said to me. "Give Rock Eater that four-year-old black."

I did so. Then she got together some things for his mother— a new four-point blanket, a blue, trade-cloth dress, various paints and trinkets, and lastly a lot of food. Rock Eater could hardly speak when he was leaving. Finally he managed to say, "These days here with you have been happy. I go from you, my good and generous relatives, only to meet you soon with my mother. She will cry with joy when she hears the words you send her and receives these fine presents." And they rode away across the bottom and over the ice-bound river.

CHAPTER 15

A Raid by the Crows

A BIG Chinook wind in the latter part of February cleared the river of ice, and the little snow in the coulées soon melted away. Grass showed green in the bottom lands in March.

One evening a vast herd of buffalo had been discovered two or three miles back from the river—a herd so large that it was said the valley of Cow Creek and the hills on each side of it were black with them as far as one could see. Soon after sunrise many hunters, with their women following on travois horses, had gone out to run this herd and get meat. An hour or so later they charged in among them on their trained runners, splitting the herd in such a way that about a thousand or more broke straight down the valley toward the camp, for the nearer to camp the killing was done the easier it was to pack in the meat. Down the valley the frightened animals fled, followed by their pursuers. We in camp heard the thunder of hoofs and saw the cloud of dust before the animals came in sight. Our lodges were pitched on the lower side of the bottom, between the creek and a steep, bare, rocky ridge. Every man, woman, and child of us had hurried outside to witness the chase.

It was really far more exciting to see such a run near at

hand than to take part in it. First of all, the huge, shaggy, oddly shaped beasts charged madly by with a thunderous pounding of hoof and rattle of horns, causing the ground to tremble as if from an earthquake; and then the hunters, their long hair streaming in the wind, guiding their trained mounts here and there in the thick of it all, singling out this fat cow or that choice young bull, firing their guns or leaning over and driving an arrow deep into the vital part of the great beast. The plain over which they passed became dotted with the dead, with great animals standing head down, swaying, staggering, as the life blood flowed from mouth and nostrils, finally crashing over on the ground, limp and lifeless heaps.

That is what we, standing by our lodges, saw that morning. No one cheered the hunters, nor spoke, nor laughed. It was too solemn a moment. We saw death abroad; huge, powerful beasts, full of tireless energy, suddenly stricken into so many heaps of meat and hide. Paradoxical as it may seem, the Blackfeet reverenced, regarded as "medicine," or sacred, these animals which they killed for food, whose hides furnished them with shelter and clothing.

A band of horses drinking at the river became frightened at the noise of the approaching herd. They bounded up the bank and raced out over the bottom, heads and tails up, running directly toward the herd, which swerved to the eastward, crossed the creek, and came tearing down our side of it. The rocky ridge hemming in the bottom was too steep for them to climb, so they kept on in the flat directly toward the lodges. Some in their terror ran wildly around, stopping behind one lodge a moment, then running to the shelter of another. Women screamed, children bawled, men shouted words of advice and command.

I seized hold of Nät-ah'-ki, ran with her over to one of Berry's wagons, and got her up in it. In a moment both his and Sorrel Horse's wagons were filled with people, others crouching under and standing in lines behind them. Persons in the vicinity of the ridge clambered up among the rocks. Those near the creek jumped onto it, but many stood helplessly behind their lodges in the center of the camp.

Now, the leaders of the herd reached the outer edge of the village. They could not draw back, for those behind forced them forward, and they loped on, threading their way between the lodges, nimbly jumping from side to side to avoid them, kicking out wickedly at them as they passed. For all his great size and uncouth shape, the buffalo was quick and active on his feet.

I had taken shelter behind one of the wagons with many others and watched the brown, living stream surge by, winding in and out between the lodges as a river winds past the island and bars in its channel. We held our breath anxiously, for we well knew that almost anything—the firing of a gun or sight of some suspicious object ahead—might throw the herd into confusion. If it turned or bunched up in a compact mass, people would surely be trampled to death, lodges overturned, the greater part of camp reduced to ruin. Finally the last of the herd passed beyond the outer lodges into the river and across it to the opposite side.

No one had been hurt, not a lodge had been overturned. But long scaffolds of drying meat, many hides and pelts of various animals pegged out on the ground to dry, had either disappeared or been cut into small fragments. That, indeed, was an experience to be remembered; we were thankful to have escaped with our lives. When we thought what would have happened had we got in the way of the rushing herd, we shuddered.

The next day the trees and high bushes bordering the river were bright with the people's offerings to their Sun god. They gave always their best, their choicest and most prized ornaments and finery.

One warm, sunny day in the end of March, camp was broken, and crossing the wide, shallow ford of the river at Cow Island, we climbed the south slope of the valley and strung out over the plain. At such times Nät-ah'-ki and I frequently dropped behind and rode along a mile or more to the right or left of the

trail on little side hunts. We were free to do this, for mother
and her uncle's family took charge of our pack and travois
horses, and herded them along with their own. And when we
came to camp in the evening we would find our lodge put up,
the couches made, wood and water at hand, the tireless mother
sitting by the fire awaiting our arrival. Sometimes Nät-ah'-ki
would remonstrate with her for doing all this, but she would
always say, "Young people should be happy. This my mother
did for me when I was newly married. Some day you will likely
be doing it for your daughter." Which remark would cause my
woman to turn away in confusion, and she would pretend to
be very busy about something. Alas! they thought that this
carefree life was going to last forever. Even we white men little
dreamed how soon the buffalo were to disappear.

On this lovely morning we rode gradually, slowly and
obliquely away to the west until we were a couple of miles from
the trail. Still farther out we could see several hunters now
and then, as they passed over a rise of ground, and occasionally
the long column of the moving camp was in sight. Sometimes
we loitered, letting our horses feed as they walked, and again
we would start them into a lope and keep it up until we were
well abreast of the others. Nät-ah'-ki kept up a ceaseless chat-
ter of gossip and story and questions about the country from
which I had come.

Along toward noon we came to the head of a pine-clad coulée
running into the far-away Judith, and in a little grove there
was a small spring of clear, cold water. We drank, and then
leading our animals up to the top of the slope where we could
obtain a good view of the surrounding country we ate our lunch
of bread, depuyer, and dried meat. A fox cub came trotting over
the bench opposite us, ran down the slope into the grove and
to the spring, and presently came out on our side, sniffing the
air, undoubtedly having scented our food. It walked up to
within thirty feet of us, stopped and stared at us and the grazing
horses, then circled around and finally stretched out on its
belly, head up watching us intently, and frequently sniffing

the air, curiously working its slender, delicately contoured nose.

"Did I ever tell you," Nät-ah'-ki asked, "about my grandfather and his pet fox? No? Well then, listen.

"One night my grandfather's dream commanded him to catch a cub fox, tame it, and be kind to it. He thought long over this, and counseled with others as to its meaning, but none could understand it any more than he. The next night his dream told him the same things, and again on the third night, and lastly on the fourth night. Four times his dreams commanded him. Four is the sacred number. When he arose the fourth morning, he knew that he must obey his dream. He no longer asked why, or what was meant, but after eating he went out to catch a fox. There were many foxes. Every little way as he walked he saw them running or sitting by their dens into which they disappeared as he drew near. He had a long lariat, to an end of which he had tied a length of fine buckskin string. Making a running noose of the string, he would lay it in a circle around the entrance to the den, then go back as far as the lariat extended and lie down to watch for the animals. If one poked its head out, he would jerk the lariat, and the noose would tighten around its neck or body. Children catch ground squirrels in this way—he had done it himself in youthful days—and he believed that in like manner he would capture a fox.

"These animals have more than one entrance to their den, often as many as five or six. If my grandfather set the noose around a hole into which he saw a fox go, the animal was certain to look out from another opening, and seeing him lying nearby, would dodge back and appear no more, even though he waited a long time.

Thus passed the first day, and the second. On the evening of the third he noosed one, but with a snap of its sharp teeth the fox cut the string and escaped. Tired and thirsty, and hungry, he was returning home that evening, when on the side of a coulée he saw five young foxes playing near the entrance to their den, the mother and father sitting nearby watching them.

They were very small, so young that they tumbled over each other slowly and awkwardly. He sat down on the opposite side of the coulée and watched them until the sun set and night came on. Over and over he asked himself how he could catch one of the young. He prayed, too, calling upon the gods, upon his dream, to show him the way.

"Returning to his lodge, he ate and drank and filled and lighted his pipe, again praying for help. And suddenly, as he sat there silently smoking, the way was shown him. The gods had taken pity on him. He went to bed and slept well. 'Go out and find a large buffalo shoulder blade,' he said to my grandmother, after the morning meal, 'then take a cowskin and accompany me.'

"They went to the den of young foxes. Very close to the place where the little ones played was a large bunch of rye grass, and in the center of it my grandfather began to cut away the sod, to loosen the earth with his knife. My grandmother helped him, using the shoulder blade as a white man does his shovel, removing the earth and piling it on the cowskin, then carrying the load away and scattering it in the bottom of the coulée. They worked and worked, cutting and digging, and scraping, until the hole was deep enough for my grandfather to stand in. His eyes were even with the top of the ground, the fringe of rye grass still standing made a good screen. The foxes might scent him, but they could not see him. 'Go home,' he said to my grandmother when they had finished their work. 'Go home and make a sacrifice to the Sun and pray that I may succeed in that which I have to do.'

"Then he got into the hole and stood very still, waiting, watching for the little ones to come out. Long he waited. The sun seemed to travel very slowly down toward the mountains. It was very hot. He became very thirsty. His legs ached, but he stood as motionless as the ground itself, always watching. A little while before sunset an old fox came out, and walked halfway around the rye grass bunch. Then, suddenly, it scented him, and ran swiftly away up the coulée. Soon afterward the little ones came forth, one by one, slowly and lazily, yawning and stretching themselves, blinking their eyes in the strong light. They began to play, as they had done on the previous evening, and before long they gathered in a scuffle at the edge of the rye grass. Then my grandfather quickly reached out, and seized one by the back of the neck. 'Hai-ya', little brother,' he cried, 'I have caught you.' Climbing out of the hole he wrapped the cub in a fold of his robe and hurried to his lodge. He was happy. Four times his dream had spoken to him. On the fourth day he had fulfilled its command. He felt sure that in some way the taking of the fox was to be for his good.

"Puh'-po-kan—dream—my grandfather named the little animal. From the very beginning it had no fear of him, and soon made friends with the dogs of the lodge. The fox ate readily the bits of meat my grandfather gave it, and learned to drink water and soup. Grandfather forbade anyone to pet it, or feed it, or call it by name, so it was friendly only with him. It wanted to follow him wherever he went, and at night would crawl under the robes and sleep beside him. It was such a funny little one, always wanting to play with my grandfather or with the lodge dogs. When it was frightened by anything it would run to him, making short, gasping, hoarse little barks, just as we hear them at night out beyond the lodges. I did so want to play with it, take it up in my arms and pet it, but always my mother would say, 'Don't you dare do it; it's a sacred one, and if you touch it something dreadful will happen to you. Perhaps you would go blind.'

"Not a mouse wandered in under the lodge-skin but Puh'-po-kan had found and killed it, and often he would bring home a bird or ground squirrel. When Puh'-po-kan had seen two winters, we were camping on the Little River, just north of the Bear's Paw Mountains. One night, after the lodge fires had all died out and everyone was asleep, Puh'-po-kan awoke my grandfather by backing up against his head and barking in a way it had when frightened. 'Stop that,' said my grandfather, reaching up and giving the little one a light slap. 'Stop barking and go to sleep.'

"But Puh'-po-kan would not stop. Instead he barked harder

than ever, trembling because he was so excited. My grandfather raised up on his elbow and looked around. The moon was shining down through the smoke-hole, so that he could make out the different objects in the lodge. Over by the doorway there was something that did not belong there, a dark motionless object that looked like a person crouching. 'Who are you?' he asked. 'What do you want here?'

"No answer.

"Then my grandfather spoke again: 'Tell me quickly who you are. Get up and talk, or I will shoot you.'

"Still there was no answer. Puh'-po-kan kept on barking. My grandfather quietly reached out for his gun, which lay at the head of his bed, cocked it without noise, aimed and fired it. With a fearful scream a man sprang up and fell dead right in the hot ashes and coals of the fire-place, from which my grandfather quickly dragged him.

"A fire was quickly built and the light showed that the dead man was an enemy, a Sioux. He had no weapon except a long knife, still firmly gripped in his right hand. When the fox gave warning of his presence, he most likely thought that by remaining crouched on the ground he would not be discovered, and that those aroused would soon again fall asleep. He seemed to have come to the camp alone, for no trace of others could be found, no horses were stolen.

"All the talk in camp was about the fox, and my grandfather's dream. It was all great medicine. And my grandfather—how pleased he was! He made many sacrifices, prayed much, and loved Puh'-po-kan more than ever. Two more winters the little one lived, and then one summer night it was bitten by a rattlesnake and soon died. The women wrapped the swollen little body in robes and buried it on a scaffold they made in a cottonwood tree, just as if it had been a person."

I recinched our saddles. Nät-ah'-ki spread the remains of our lunch on a smooth flat stone. "Eat heartily, little brother," she said. We mounted and rode away, and looking back we saw the fox busily chewing a piece of meat.

Late in the afternoon we arrived in camp, which had been

pitched near a small lake on the high plateau. The water was bad, but drinkable when made into tea. In the evening I was invited to a feast given by Big Lake. Rising Wolf was also a guest, along with a number of other staid and sober men. Young men seldom feasted and smoked with their elders, and in the camp were many coteries, or social sets, just as we find them in any civilized community, with the exception that there was no jealousy nor rivalry between them; no one of them felt that its members were in any way better than the members of another set.

We had smoked but one pipe, when a young man hurried in through the doorway, and said: "A war party of many men is near us."

"Ah!" all exclaimed, and then Big Lake: "Quick! tell us."

"I was hunting," said the young man, "and tied my horse to a bunch of sage while I crept up to a band of antelope. He got loose and ran away on his back trail and I started back afoot. At sundown I came to the top of a ridge and could see our camp, and over on another ridge near the Judith I saw at least fifty men. Saw them climb up and stand on its summit. They must have discovered our camp by the smoke from the lodge fires. I waited until it was dark, and hurried in. They will raid our horses tonight."

"Scatter out through camp, all of you," said Big Lake, quickly. "Tell the men to come here at once, warn the women not to scream or cry or run. Hurry!"

I went home and told Nät-ah'-ki the news, removed the cover of my rifle, and filled my coat pockets with cartridges. "Wait!" she said, grasping the barrel. "What are you going to do?"

"Why, Big Lake told us to meet at his lodge," I explained. "He has some good plan, I suppose."

"Yes, he is wise," she agreed, "but you are not going out there to be killed by a war party. Stay here with me."

"But our horses! I cannot remain here in the lodge and let the enemy run them off."

"They do not matter. Let them go."

"But," I said, "if I remained here people would call me a

coward, they would say to you: 'Your white man has a woman's heart; why don't you make some dresses for him?'"

That ended the argument. She just sat down on the couch, covered her head with a shawl, and thus I left her.

Big Lake was a born tactician. In the few moments required to assemble the men he had thought out his plan of defense, and issued his orders in a few words. The various bands of the All Friends Society were told off into four groups, out to the north, south, east, and west of camp, and there they would await the arrival of the enemy. All others not of the society were to go with any one of the bands they chose. It was not feared that a war party would make an attack on camp. They came, of course, to steal horses, and the plan was to go out where the herds were grazing and lie in wait. The really valuable animals were all tethered, as usual, near the lodges of their owners, and passing by the herds of common horses, the enemy would try to get in to them, cut their ropes and lead them away.

With the Crazy Dogs and Raven Carriers I moved out with thirty or forty others who, like myself, belonged to no organization. We spread out in a wide line, and after walking slowly and silently for about half a mile, word was passed to stop, whereupon we sat down in the cover of the sage and greasewood brush. The moon was low in the western sky and due to set about midnight, so it was not very dark; we could see quite plainly the brush forty or fifty yards distant. The man nearest me on the right slowly crawled over and sat beside me.

"The night light is about to go out of sight," he whispered. "The war party will appear soon, if they come at all."

He spoke truly, for a little later we heard away out beyond, a murmur of voices. Then there was silence, and then with soft tread and harsh swish of brush against their leggings, the raiders came into view, unsuspectingly advancing. Someone on my left fired first, and then the whole line shot an irregular volley. Sparks of the cheap black powder glowed and sparkled as they spouted from fuke and rifle into the darkness. The flashes blinded us for a moment, and when we could see again the enemy were running away. They had fired a number of shots in answer to ours, but as we afterward found, not one of their bullets had hit any of us.

Almost as one man our line sprang forward. Here were bodies, five of them, and one with life still in it. Thud went a war club and the recumbent figure sprawled out, face up, in the waning moonlight. In a trice the dead were scalped, their arms taken by those who first came to them. On sped our party, an occasional shot was fired at a dimly seen retreating figure. Behind us now came the three other divisions of the camp, shouting words of encouragement. But no enemy could be seen or heard, and our party stopped; it was useless to look further in the darkness.

Big Lake came up. "Spread out," he said, "spread out again and encircle the camp. Perhaps some of them are concealed in the brush closer in, and with daylight we will find them."

I shouldered my rifle and went home. Nät-ah'-ki was sitting up with her mother for company and I related all that had occurred.

"Why did you come back?" she asked, after I had finished. "Why didn't you stay out there with the rest as Big Lake ordered?"

"Hai-yah!" I exclaimed. "How peculiar are women; one may not understand them. You begged me this evening to remain here with you. I came back because I am tired and hungry, and sleepy, and now you are displeased because I returned. Well, to please you I'll go back and sit with the others until morning ·

"Sit down, crazy man," she said, pushing me back on the couch from which I had started to rise. "You will stay right there. Here is your pipe; fill it and smoke while I broil some meat and make tea."

"You are the chief," I said to her, contentedly leaning back against a willow mat. "It shall be as you say."

CHAPTER 16

Nät-ah'-ki's Wedding

AT daylight an unusual stir and confusion in camp awoke us, and Nät-ah'-ki went out to learn what it was all about. She soon returned with the news that our enemy of the night proved to be Crows, that the bodies of seven in all had been found, and that they had succeeded in running off seventy or more horses. A large party had already started in pursuit, and we were to break camp until they returned. I arose and dressed, had breakfast, and went visiting.

Turning into Weasel Tail's lodge I found him nursing a gash in the thigh, where a Crow bullet had creased him. I sat with him while many other visitors came and went. All were calling the Crows any bad name their language contained, but in this line their speech was exceedingly limited. The very best they could do was to call their enemy dog faces and present them to the Sun, begging him to destroy them.

I went on to the lodge of the chief, where I found many of the principal men assembled. "I for one," Big Lake was saying when I entered, "will talk against making peace with the Crows so long as I live. Let us all agree never to smoke their tobacco.

Let us teach our children that they are like the rattlesnake,
always to be killed on sight."

The visitors heartily agreed to this, and they kept their word,
sending party after party against their Yellowstone enemies
until the Government put a stop to inter-tribal war. The last
raid occurred in the summer of 1885.

There was much scalp-dancing during the day, participated
in by those who had most recently lost a relative in battle with
the Crows. This was not, as has been often luridly pictured, a
spectacular dance of fierce exultation and triumph over the
death of their enemy. As performed by the Blackfeet, it was a
solemn spectacle. Those participating in it blackened their
faces, hands, and moccasins with charcoal, and wore their
meanest, plainest clothes. An aged man held the scalp of the
enemy tied to a willow wand in front of him, and the others
ranged in line on each side. Then they sang a plaintive song
in a minor key. On this occasion there were seven scalps, seven
parties dancing in different parts of camp at once, and one band
of mourners after another took their turn, so that the performance lasted until night.

The pursuing party returned at dusk, having failed to overtake the enemy. Some were for starting at once on a raid into
the Crow country, but there was now little ammunition in camp
and it was decided that we should push on to Fort Benton with
as little delay as possible. After obtaining a good supply of
powder and ball there, the war party could turn back southward. Four or five days later camp was pitched in the big
bottom opposite the Fort. Nät-ah'-ki and I crossed the river,
and wended our way to the little adobe house. There we found
Berry, his wife and mother, and the good Crow Woman. What
a happy lot they were, those women, as they bustled around
and got in each other's way trying to get supper ready. And I
am sure Berry and I were happy too. We did not say much as
we stretched out on a buffalo-robe lounge and smoked, but it
was all good enough for us, and each knew that the other felt
so.

In the evening Berry and I went down to the Fort for a while, and, of course, we called in at Keno Bill's place. As usual, at that time of year, the town was full of traders and trappers, bull-whackers and mule-skinners, miners and Indians, all awaiting the arrival of the steamboats which were soon due to arrive. Every table in Keno's place was so crowded with players that one couldn't edge in to watch a game. Keno himself and two assistants were busy behind the bar, as the kegs still held out despite the heavy draught on them during the winter months. There were even a few bottles of beer left. I gladly paid a dollar and four bits for one of them, and Berry helped me drink it.

We went into the Overland Hotel for a moment on our way home, and there among other guests I saw a man who I thought was a preacher; at any rate, a white tie adorned his blue-flannel shirt front, and he wore a black coat. I went up to him and said: "Excuse me, sir, but I'd like to know if you are a preacher?"

"I am," he replied with a pleasant smile. "I am a minister of the Methodist Episcopal Church. I have been in the mountains for the past year, preaching and mining, and am now on my way to my home in the States."

"Well," I continued, "if you'll go along with me I guess I can find a job for you."

He arose at once. "May I ask," he said on the way, "what is to be the nature of my services? A baptism or marriage, or is there some sick one in need of a few words?"

"It's a marriage," I replied; "that is, providing the other party is willing."

The women were gaily talking and laughing when we arrived, but, as always before strangers, they became silent at once. I called Nät-ah'-ki into the back room. "He out there," I said to her, "is a sacred (a Sun) white man. I have asked him to marry us."

"Oh," she cried. "How did you know my wish? It is what I have always wanted you to do, but I—I was afraid, ashamed to ask it of you. But is he a real sacred white man? He wears no black robe, no cross?"

"He is of another society," I replied. "There are a thousand of them, and each claims that his is the only true one. It matters not to us. Come on."

And so, Berry acting as interpreter, we were married and we sent the preacher forth with a gold piece as a souvenir of the occasion....

"I'm hungry," said Berry, "broil us a couple of buffalo tongues, you women."

Broiled tongue and bread, tea and apple sauce comprised the wedding feast, and that also was good enough.

"It is this," Nät-ah'-ki confided to me later. "Many white men who have married women of our tribe according to our customs, have used them only as playthings and then have left them. But those who took women by the words of a sacred white man, have never left them. I know that *you* would never leave me. But how the others have laughed at me, joked about me, saying: 'Crazy girl, you love your man, and you are a fool; he has not married you in the white man's way, and will leave you as soon as he sees another woman with a prettier face.' They can never say that again. No, never."

We had planned, Berry and I, to remain in Fort Benton during the summer and make a camp trade the following winter. The steamboats began to arrive in May and then the levee was a busy place. The traders were also rushed, the Indians crowding in to dispose of the last of their robes and furs. But we had no part in this, and in a few weeks we became restless.

We returned to the Fort and began to plan for the winter's trade and to make lists of the goods needed. Whether we should make a camp trade, or build a post, and at what point, would depend entirely on the Indians' plans for the winter.

CHAPTER 17

The War Trip of Queer Person

BERRY saddled a horse one morning and rode out to the camp on the Marias to interview the chiefs. When he returned, a day or two later, he was more than satisfied with the result of the council, for it was agreed that the winter should be passed on the Marias. We could use the post that had been built two years previously. It needed some repairs, but by the middle of September we were well established there, with a good stock of goods. The chief difficulty in moving out was our inability to keep the bull-whackers sober. One of them, Whisky Lyons, never was on hand to help load the wagons, and when we were ready to pull out we had to hunt him up, tie a rope under his arms and souse him in the river until he came to his senses. There was another, Captain George, whose specialty was a singing spree. He had a large store of quaint songs, which he would sing unendingly when drunk.

I have often wondered whatever became of the oldtime bull-whackers, they who spent their money so freely and joyously whenever they had the opportunity. I never heard of them dying. I never saw them after the advent of the railroads and the close of transportation on the upper Missouri. They simply vanished.

There was little for us to do until the prime winter robes began to come in. The Piegans had moved out on Milk River back of the Sweetgrass Hills, and would not return to stay until cold weather drove them in. We missed Sorrel Horse, who had gone down on the Missouri somewhere below the mouth of the Judith, to run a wood yard and to trade with the Gros Ventres.

During the time of slack trade, Berry was uneasy. Always a very nervous, active man, he could not be happy unless he was doing something. I have seen him throw and shoe a bull that did not need shoeing, or repair an old wagon wheel that could never be of any service.

But if Berry was at his wit's end for something to do, it was different with me; no day was too long. Nät-ah'-ki and I went hunting, either in the river bottoms for deer, or out on the plains for antelope. Buffalo, of course, were everywhere; and down below the post some ten or twelve miles there were numbers of big-horn. And the evenings were as full of interest as the days. My dingy old notebooks contain the outlines of those happy times, and as I look over them it all comes back to me as vividly as if it all had happened yesterday.

Here, for instance, is a story the Crow Woman related one evening which may interest you as much as it did me. She called it the "Story of Three Stabs."

"In all the village there were none poorer than White Flying and her young grandson. Her man was long since dead. Her son-in-law had been killed by the Sioux, and her daughter, working in their little plantation one day, had suddenly dropped to the ground and died. The boy was still too young to go on the hunt, so they lived on what small store of corn they could raise, and what portions of meat were given them by the kindhearted. There were days when they went to bed hungry, for their best friends sometimes forgot to provide for them, and White Flying was too proud to go out and beg. When this happened, the boy would say, 'Never mind, grandmother, wait until I grow up and I'll kill more meat than you can take care of.'

"The boy's name was Sees Black, a name an old medicine

man had given him when he was born. No one but his grandmother called him that—he was nicknamed Queer Person, for
he had ways different from those of any other boy ever heard
of. He never played with other children, never laughed or cried,
and scarcely spoke to anyone except his grandmother. He
seemed to be dreaming all the time and would sit on the bank
of the river, or on the hill near the village, often for half a day,
looking straight away into the distance as if he saw there things
of great interest—so great that he never noticed people who
passed near him. He brought strange and forbidden things to
his lodge, once, a human skull, which he placed under the end
of his couch. When making up his bed one day, the old woman
found it, and it frightened her so that she fell down and was
dead for a while. When she came to life, she begged him to take
it back to the place where he had found it. He did so at once,
for he was a good boy and always obeyed her. When she asked
him why he had taken it he replied, 'I am seeking a great
medicine. I thought that if I slept by it I might have a powerful
dream.'

"Sometimes he would leave the village and stay away all
night. When his grandmother asked him where he had been,
he would tell her that he had gone upon the plain, or down in
the timber, or out on a sandbar, to sleep, hoping that some of
the spirits or animals who wander about in the darkness would
have pity and give him the medicine he sought.

"While other boys of his age still played, he made bows and
arrows. He watched the flint workers, and became as skillful
as they in chipping out sharp, thin arrow points. He hunted,
too; at first, rabbits in the rosebush thickets; and then, one day,
he brought home a fine deer—a part of the meat at a time—
which he had shot on a trail they used in going to and from
their watering place. After that he seldom hunted rabbits, but
often brought in deer, and once in a while the hide and meat
of a buffalo which he crept up on and killed in a coulée, or at
the river where they went to drink. Still, they were very poor.
All the family horses had long since been given the doctors
who had tried to cure the grandfather. Without horses Queer

Person could not go out on the big hunts and bring in loads of meat sufficient to last during the bad weather, or through the long sieges of the Sioux against them.

"The summers and the winters passed. The boy grew and grew, tall and strong, and very fine-looking. He was now old enough to go to war, to fight the enemy and drive away their horses. But no war party would let him join them. 'One who slept with skulls,' they said, 'who went forth to sleep where the ghosts wandered—there is surely something wrong with such a person; he will cause bad luck to befall us.'

"Of course, the young man grieved much about this, and the grandmother grieved with him. And then he became angry. 'I will make them take back their words,' he said to the old woman. 'I will go against the enemy by myself, and the time shall come when they will beg to go with me. Make me a boat and I'll float down the river to the camps of the Sioux.'

"White Flying went out and cut the willows, crossed and recrossed them, bent them to the proper shape, then stretched and bound upon the frame the fresh hide of a big bull, and the boat was done. It was not like the boats of the white men. It was flat on the bottom and round, like the tubs white people have for washing clothes. Unless one was accustomed to them he was helpless, for if he did not upset when he tried to paddle, he would only make the boat whirl around and around like a child's top, and it would drift wherever the current and the wind chose to push it.

"There was a full moon now, and one night when it rose, soon after the sun had gone down, Queer Person got into his boat and pushed it out from the shore. No one was there to see him leave, except his grandmother. No one else in the village knew that he was going away.

"The poor old woman sat down on the shore, covered her head with her robe, and cried, cried for those loved ones who were dead, and for the young man who was going, perhaps, to join them and leave her alone in her old age.

"On and on Queer Person drifted in the bright moonlight, down the wide, deep river, never paddling except to keep facing down stream and to avoid the snags and sandbars. The beavers played and splashed around him, and he prayed to them. 'Pity me,' he said; 'give me of your cunning, so that I may escape all danger.'

"Where the water boiled and swirled under the shadow of a high-cut bank, some dim thing rose above the surface, and slowly sank and disappeared. He could not see it plainly. It might have been one of the people who live in the dark, deep places. He prayed to them also, and dropped a sacrifice to them. 'Do not harm me,' he said; 'let me pass over your waters in safety.'

"Thus the night passed, and with the daylight he went to the shore, dragging his boat into some thick willows and then smoothing off the trail he had made across the sands.

"Thus drifting by night and hiding in the daytime, Queer Person kept on toward the country of the Sioux. Every morning, after going ashore, he would walk out to the edge of the timber, sometimes climbing a slope, and look carefully up and down the valley for signs of people. He saw none until the fifth morning, when he discovered a great camp directly across the river in a big bottom. There was a long strip of cottonwoods bordering the stream. The lodges were pitched on the open plain back of it. A large number of horses were tied in the camp, people were just coming out and turning them loose to graze. 'My medicine is good,' he said to himself. 'I have come safely down the river, and here I am in sight of that which I seek.'

"During the day he slept for some time, feeling quite safe where he was, for the enemy had no boats, the river was very high, and they could not cross. He made plans for the night. Toward evening he slept again, and then his dream helped him and showed him the way to make a great name for himself.

"This is what he did. Listen to the cunning his dream gave him: in the night he crossed the river, put some stones in his boat, then cut a hole in the bottom, so that it filled with water and sank. Then he went into the timber and buried his things beside a large cottonwood log, buried his clothes, moccasins, weapons. Nothing remained on him, except his belt and breech-clout. Lastly, he unbound his braided hair, washed it to straighten out the kinks, then tangled it and scattered dust in it. He smeared mud and dust on his body, soiled his breech-clout, scratched his legs with a rose bush. When he had done, he looked very wild, very poor. He went out of the timber, down to the lower end of the bottom, and remained there the rest of the night.

"When the sun came up and people were moving about, Queer Person arose and walked toward the camp, sometimes stopping and looking around, sometimes running, again walking slowly, looking at the ground. Thus he approached the lodges, and the great crowd of people who stood staring at him. He pretended not to see them, walking straight on. They parted to let him pass and then followed him.

"He stopped by a fire outside a lodge, upon which some meat was roasting, and sat down. The women tending it fled. The people gathered around him and stood and talked. Of course, they thought him crazy. A man came up, asked him many questions in signs; he did not reply, except occasionally to point down the river. This man had a wide scar on his left cheek. Queer Person knew that he was a chief. He had heard his people talk about him as a terrible man in battle. After a time an old woman came and set some broiled meat before him. He seized it and ate it as if he had been starving for many days. He ate a great deal, and a long time.

"The people mostly went away to their lodges. The scar-faced man made signs again, but when he got no answer he took Queer Person by the arm, made him get up, and led him to his lodge, showed him a couch, made signs that it was his, that he should live in the lodge. Still the young man pretended not to understand, but he remained there, going out sometimes but always returning. People made him presents—moccasins, leggings, a buckskin shirt, a cow-skin robe. He put them on and wore them. After a few days he would walk about in camp, and the people would hardly notice him.

"Queer Person discovered that the scar-faced chief was a very cruel man. He had five wives, the first one older than he, and very ugly. The others were all young women and good-looking. The old wife abused the others and made them do all the work. Sometimes she struck them, often the chief would beat them or seize a couple and knock their heads together. The young man could not help but look often at the youngest one. She was so pretty and so sad. He met her often in the grove when she gathered wood and they would smile at each other. After many days, he found her all alone in the woods one evening. His time had come and he quickly told her in signs who he was, that he was not crazy, that he had started all alone to war. And then he said that he loved her. He asked if she would go away with him and be his woman. She did not answer, but she clung to him and kissed him. Then they heard someone coming and they parted.

"The next day they met again in the timber and hid in the thicket willows and made their plans to leave.

"When the fire had died out and the chief and his old wife snored, Queer Person and the young woman crept out of the lodge and went to the river. There they tied together two small logs and placed their clothes upon them, on top of a little pile of brush. The young man got his clothes and weapons which he had buried, and piled them there too. Then, with nothing but his knife, he went back to the lodge, leaving the woman by the raft. He crept to the chief's couch, raised his knife and gave him one deep stab right in the heart, then another and another. The man did not cry out, but he kicked a little and the old woman beside him awoke. Queer Person at once seized her by the throat and strangled her until she lay still. Then he scalped the chief, took his weapons, and ran back to the raft. The woman was waiting for him, and together they waded out, pushing the logs, and when they got into deep water they swam, holding on to the logs with one hand. Thus they crossed the river and dressed and started on the long walk to the Arickaree village. In the camp from which they had come, all was quiet. The trouble there had not yet been discovered.

"What a proud old woman White Flying was when her grandson returned home with his pretty wife, with the scalp and the weapons of the terrible chief. He had made a great name. In time he himself would be a chief. And he did become one, the head chief of his people. No one any longer called him Queer Person. He took the name Three Stabs, and all were proud to call him that. He and his good wife lived to great age. They had many children and were happy."

CHAPTER 18

A Wolverine's Medicine

WE camped with Weasel Tail, whose good woman spread out a number of new robes for our use. Visitors came and went, and we were called to several smokes at different places. In the latter part of the evening, after the feasting and visiting was over, Weasel Tail and Talks-with-the-buffalo, the two inseparables, and I were again together, as we had been on many a previous night. We would sit together for hours, smoking when we felt like it, talking or idly silent, as the mood struck us. The women passed around some berry pemmican, which was fine. "Friend," said Talks-with-the-buffalo, after we had eaten and the pipe was again filled and lighted, "I have a present for you."

"Ah!" I replied, "I am always glad to get presents."

"Yes," he continued, "and I will be glad to get rid of this. I want you to take it tomorrow morning, lest something happen that you never get the thing. It is a wolverine skin. Listen and I will tell you what trouble it has caused me. First, the way I got it: one morning my woman told me to kill some bighorn. She wanted their skins for a dress. I said that those animals were too difficult to get, that she ought to make her dress of antelope skins, which also make fine soft leather when well tanned. But they would not do. They were uneven, thick on the neck, too thin on the belly. Nothing would do but bighorn skins, because they were all of the right kind—neither thick nor very thin in any place. I tried to get out of it by saying that if she must have them I would require her to go on the hunt with me, and help pack down what I killed. I thought that when I said this, she would make up her mind that antelope skins were good enough. I was mistaken. 'Of course, I'll go with you,' she said. 'Let us start in the morning.'

"I made up my mind that I would pretend to be sick; but when I awoke in the morning I had forgotten all about the hunt, and after I had got up and washed, I ate a big meal. When I did remember, it was too late. I couldn't get her to believe that I was sick, after making her broil meat twice. We started, and rode as far as our horses could carry us, up the north side of the west Sweetgrass Mountain, then we tied the animals and went on afoot. It was pretty steep climbing; in places the pines grew so closely together that we could hardly squeeze between them. My hunting partner was always behind. 'Come on, come on,' I kept saying, and 'Wait, wait for me,' she was always calling, and when she caught up she would be breathing like a horse that has run a race and sweat would drip off her chin. 'It is very pleasant, this bighorn hunting,' I told her, and she said, 'You speak the truth. Just look how high up we are, and how far we can see the plains away northward.'

"After that I did not tease her, because she had good courage, and did her best to climb. I traveled slowly, and she kept close behind me. We approached the summit. The top of that mountain—you have seen it—is a mystery place. When Old Man made the world he painted the rocks he placed there with pretty colors, red, brown, yellow and white. Some say that it is a lucky place to hunt; others, that if one kills anything there, he will have bad luck of some kind. I thought of this as I climbed, and at last I stopped and spoke to my woman. I told her that we had, perhaps, better go back on account of the bad luck we might have if I made a killing there. But she just laughed and laughed, and said that I was getting to be very foolish.

"'Well,' I said to her, 'if you must laugh, do so with your hand over your mouth, else you will scare everything on this mountain.'

"We continued climbing, and in a little while came to the summit. Looking out at it from the cover of some pines, I saw a band of bighorn, maybe twenty or more, all she ones, and their young, except a two-year-old male. I took a careful aim at him—he was close by and standing side to me—and as it was handy, I rested my gun on a limb of a tree. I took a very good aim, right for his heart, and fired. I don't know where the bullet went, but I am sure that it never hit him, for we could find neither hair no blood where he had stood nor along his trail. When I shot, the smoke hung like a little cloud before me, and when it blew away I saw the animals, just as they disappeared into the timber down the slope. I was much surprised that I had not killed the animal, most surprised when I found that I had not even hit him, for I had aimed so long and so carefully.

"'You must have hit him,' said my woman. 'Let us look again. We will likely find him lying dead somewhere far away.'

"We followed his trail for some distance down in the timber; it was easy to follow, for his track was larger than that of the others; but there was no sign at all that he was hurt. We climbed up on top again, and sat down at the edge of the bare rocks, in the shelter of a low pine. I thought that if we stayed here a while some more bighorn might come along. But none appeared, although we sat and watched until long after the middle of the day. We were about to leave, when a big wolverine appeared, walking among the rocks, smelling and snuffing.

"He looked very pretty, his hair just shining in the sun. He soon came near, and the next time he climbed upon a rock I shot him. He fell off it and hardly kicked. I told my woman to skin it carefully. She said that she would tan it very soft, and we would make you a present of it. The bad luck began right there. She cut her hand—the knife slipped—before she had half got the hide off, and I had to finish the work. Then we started homeward.

"When we got to the horses I tied the skin behind my saddle and got astride. The horse had been standing with his head to the wind, and when I turned him he got the scent of the wolverine for the first time, and it frightened him so that he went crazy. He snorted and made a big jump down the mountain, and when he struck, the jar threw me off, right on my back into a lot of stones. I thought I was broken in two. The horse went on, jumping, and kicking and snorting, right into a pile of big rocks, where he got caught by a foreleg, and broke it.

"As soon as I got my breath and could walk and my woman found my gun I had to go down and shoot him. We were late getting home, for we rode double on the other horse, and had to hang on it my saddle and other things. We had learned it was bad luck to kill anything on the painted rocks.

"It was some days before I recovered from the soreness caused by my fall. My woman could not tan the wolverine skin on account of her sore hand, so she got a widow to do it. The next morning the old woman brought back the skin. 'Take it,' she said. 'I have been sick all night, and in my dream a wolverine came and tried to bite me. It is bad medicine. I will not tan it.'

"You know old Beaver Woman? Yes? We gave the skin to her. She said that she wasn't afraid of wolverines, that her medicine was stronger than theirs. Well, she took it to her lodge and went to work, fleshed it, put on the liver and brains, rolled it up and laid it away for two or three days. When it was well soaked with the mixture, she cleaned it and began to dry it, working it over the sinew cord, when she suddenly fell over dead for a short time. When she came to life her mouth was drawn around to one side and she could hardly speak. She was that way about four nights. Of course, the skin came back to us. The cut on my woman's hand had healed, so she went to work and finished the tanning, and without any mishap.

"Day before yesterday we started to move in; my woman packed the skin with other things on the lodge-skin horse.

When we made camp in the evening, the skin was missing. Everything else that had been placed in the pack was there, the skin only was gone. While we were wondering how it could have happened, a young man rode up and tossed it to us. 'I found it on the trail,' he said.

"So, you see, this skin is bad medicine. I said that I was going to give it to you, and I now do so. Also I have told you all the evil it has done. I shall not blame you if you throw it in the fire. All I ask is that you take it off our hands."

Of course, I accepted the skin. In time it became part of a handsome robe, a small bear skin in the center, the border of six wolverines.

Nät-ah'-ki and I were in the saddle next morning long before the lodges began to come down, and started homeward. It had been a very warm night. Soon after we left a light wind sprang up from the north, cold, damp, and with a strong odor of burning grass. We knew the sign well enough; the smoky smell was always the precursor of a storm from the north. "The Cold-maker is near," said Nät-ah'-ki. "Let us hurry on."

Looking back, we saw that the Sweetgrass hills had become enveloped in a dense white fog, which was sweeping southward with incredible swiftness. It soon overtook us, and was so thick that we could not see a hundred yards ahead. The sweat on our horses instantly froze; fine particles of frost filled the air; our ears began to tingle, and we covered them with handkerchiefs. It was useless to attempt to look out a course to the river, so we gave our horses the reins and kept them going, and arrived home before noon. The wind had steadily increased, the fog had gone, but snow had taken its place. Winter had come.

Prime robes soon began to come in, and we were kept busy exchanging goods and spirits for them. For convenience, we used brass checks in trading, each check representing one dollar. Having some robes to sell, an Indian would stalk in, followed by one or more of his women carrying them, and, as a rule, he would stand at a little distance, very silent and straight, his robe or blanket partly concealing his face, while we examined them and counted down the checks. Unless he

needed a gun or some such expensive article, he generally gave
his woman a part of the proceeds, and invested the rest himself
in whatever took his fancy; tobacco always, generally some
liquor. They always wanted to taste of the liquor before buying,
and we kept for that purpose a pailful of it and a cup behind
the high counter. A few moments after one of these haughty
customers had taken a drink, he became quite affable and before leaving would sometimes wish to embrace and kiss all
present, including the traders. It was not often that they were
more quarrelsome than so many white men. We did little trading after dark, most of the people preferring to come in the
morning to barter their fur and robes. I never knew a trader
who had not some especial and privileged friends, and we were
no exception to the rule. Several of these would sometimes
come and sit with us of an evening to smoke and tell stories,
and every little while either Berry or I would pass around the
cup.

CHAPTER 19

In Need of a Killing

THERE were days when the warm chinook was blowing, that simply drew us out of the Fort and away on the plain. Then Nät-ah'-ki and I would saddle a couple of horses and ride a great circle, returning home tired and hungry and ready to retire right after the evening meal, to sleep soundly through the long winter night. One fine day we were out, and along about two o'clock struck the river some five or six miles above the Fort and turned homeward down the valley. Riding along the trail through a grove of cottonwoods we met my enemy, Little Deer, in quest of beaver, as he had some traps tied to his saddle. He leered at Nät-ah'-ki, who happened to be in the lead, and scowled savagely at me as we passed. I must confess that I bent in the saddle once or twice, pretending to adjust my stirrup leather, but really furtively looking back under my arm. I was certainly afraid of him and felt relieved when I saw him disappear around a bend of the trail without turning to look back at us.

Passing through the grove we crossed an open flat, went into another piece of timber, and then out on a wide, bare bottom.

When about 200 yards from the last grove a gun boomed behind us and a bullet whizzed past my left side and kicked up the dust when it struck the ground farther on. Nät-ah'-ki shrieked, whipped up her horse and called to me to hurry, and we made pretty good time the rest of the way home. When the shot was fired I looked back and saw a thin cloud of smoke in front of some willows, but no man. It was Little Deer who had shot, of course, and he had come near hitting me. He had done just what I had always predicted he would do—attack me from behind; and from such a position as he was in it would have been folly to attempt to dislodge him.

Nät-ah'-ki was nearly speechless from terror and anger. I was angry, too, and swore that I would kill Little Deer at sight. Berry listened quietly, but made no comment until after supper, when we had quieted down.

"You see," he began, "that fish has some powerful relations in camp, and although they know well enough that he's in need of a killing, they are bound to avenge his death."

"And so I do nothing until I'm potted from an ambush?"

"No," he replied. "We've got to kill him, but it must be done in such a manner that we will never be suspected. Just lay low and we will find some way to do it."

After that day Little Deer came no more to the Fort. If he needed anything he sent someone to purchase it for him. When Nät-ah'-ki and I rode we went out on the open plain, avoiding the coulées and the timber in the valley. Sometimes, of a night, Berry and I would try to devise some way to effectively get rid of my enemy, but we never succeeded. Could I have waylaid him, or shot him from behind, as he had attempted to do to me, I would gladly have done so—one should always fight the devil with his own weapons.

It was a day in the fore part of March when Little Deer was missed from the camp. The previous morning he had gone out with some other hunters on the plains north of the river to kill some meat. They had separated finally, but late in the afternoon several of them had seen the missing man on a butte skinning a buffalo. During the night his horse returned and joined the band to which it belonged, still saddled and trailing its lariat.

Relatives of Little Deer went out and continued to search for him for several days, and at last they found him a long distance from the carcass of the buffalo he had skinned and cut up. He was lying in a coulée and the top of his head was crushed in. His wives and female relatives buried him, but the wives did not mourn; he had been very cruel to them and they were glad to be free. The meat of the buffalo he had killed had all been neatly cut up and prepared for loading on the horse. It was thought that he had left the place to kill something else and had been thrown, or that, perhaps, his horse had fallen with him and had kicked him in its struggle to rise.

Nät-ah'-ki was the first to hear of it and came running in, all excitement, her eyes sparkling, and gave me a hearty squeeze.

"Be happy," she cried. "Our enemy is dead; they have found his body; we can ride where we please and without fear."

One night my old friend whom I have variously called Bear Head and Wolverine—he took the former name after a successful battle he was in—paid us a visit. He stayed long after all the others had gone, silently smoking, preoccupied about something. Both Berry and I noticed it and spoke about it.

"He probably wants a new gun," I said, "or maybe a blanket or a new dress for his woman. Whatever it is I'll give it to him myself."

We were getting sleepy. Berry brought out a drink and handed it to him. "Well," he said, "tell us about it; what is on your mind?"

"I killed him," he replied. "I killed him and carried his body to the coulée and dropped it."

This was news indeed. We knew at once to whom he referred, none other than Little Deer. "Ah!" we both exclaimed, and waited for him to continue.

"I rode up to where he was tying his meat and got off my horse to tighten the saddle. We got to talking and he told about shooting at you. 'I don't see how I missed,' he said, 'for I took careful aim. But I'm not done. I'll kill that white man yet, and his woman shall be my woman, even if she does hate me.'

"His words made me mad. 'Kill him!' something said to me. 'Kill him, lest he kill your friend who has been so good to you.' He was bending over tying the last pieces of meat; I raised my rifle and struck him right on top of his head, and he fell forward; his shadow departed. I was glad that I did it."

He arose and prepared to leave. "Friend," I said grasping his hand and heartily shaking it, "what is mine is yours. What can I give you?"

"Nothing," he replied. "Nothing. I am not poor. But if I ever am in need then I will come and ask for help."

He went out and we closed and barred the door. "Well, I'll be damned if that isn't the best turn I ever knew an Indian to do for a white man," Berry exclaimed. "He's sure a friend worth having."

We kept what we had learned to ourselves, although I had a struggle to do so. It was years afterwards when I finally told Nät-ah'-ki about it, and when the time came that our friend did need help he got it.

We had with us that winter one Long-haired Jim, bull-whacker, whose hair fell in dark, rippling waves over his back and shoulders. When on the road or out at work in the wind he kept it braided, but in camp it was simply confined by a silk bandage bound around his head. He was very proud of it and kept it washed and combed.

Jim had made various trips, he claimed, on the Santa Fé and the Overland Trails, and had drifted up into Montana from Corinne. According to his own story, he was a great fighter, a successful gambler, but these advantages, he said, were offset by the fact that he was terribly unlucky in love. "I have set my affections on four different females in my time," he told us, "an I'll be dog-goned ef I got ary one of 'em.

"I come mighty close to it once," he continued. "She was a redhaired widow what kept a boardin' house in Council Bluffs. We rolled in there one evenin', an' as soon as we had corralled,

all hands went over to her place fer supper. As soon as I set
eyes on her I says to myself, 'That's a mighty fine figger of a
woman.' She was small, an' slim, an' freckled, with the purtiest
little turned-up, peart nose as ever happened. 'Who is she?' I
asked a feller settin' next me.

"'A widder,' he says, 'she runs this here place.'

"That settled it. I went to the wagon-boss, told him I quit,
drew my pay, an' packed my beddin' and war-sack over to her
place. The next evenin' I caught her settin' out on the steps all
by herself and walked right up to her. 'Mrs. Westbridge,' I says,
'I've sure fell in love with you. Will you marry me?'

"'Why, the idear!' she cried out. 'Jest listen to the man; an'
him a stranger. Scat! git out o' here!' An' she up an' run into
the house, an' into the kitchen, an' slammed an' locked the
door.

"That didn't make no difference to me. I wa'n't ordered to
leave the house, so I staid right on, an' put the question to her
every chanct I got, sometimes twict a day. She got so she didn't
run, took it kinder good-natured like, but she always gave me
a straight no for an answer. I wa'n't no way discouraged.

"Well, it run along a matter of two weeks, an' one evenin'
I asked her again; 'twas the twenty-first time, which number
bein' my lucky one, I considered it sure to win. An' it did.

"'Yes, sir, Mr. Jim. What's-yer-name,' she says, straight out,
'I'll marry yer on certain conditions:

"'You must cut your hair.'

"'Yep.'

"'An' throw away them six-shooters an' that long knife.'

"'Yep.'

"'An' quit gamblin.'

"'Yep.'

"'An' help me run this boardin' house.'

"Yes, I agreed to it all, an' she said we'd be married the
comin' Sunday. I asked her fer a kiss, but she slapped my face
an' run off into the kitchen. 'Never mind,' I says, settin' down
on the steps, 'I'll wait till she comes out an' ketch her.'

"Wal, sir, I was a settin' there all peaceful an' happy like, when along comes an ornery-lookin' one-leg cripple an' asks, 'Is this whar Miss Westbridge lives?'

"'It are,' I said. 'An' what might you want of her?'

"'Oh, nothing,' he says, 'cept she's my wife.'

"I allow I might have swatted him, even if he was a cripple, if the woman hadn't come out just then. When she see him she just throwed up her hands and cried out: 'My Gawd! Wherever did you come from? I thought you was dead. They told me you was. Are you sure it's you?'

"'Yes, Sairy,' he said. 'It's me all right; that is, what's left of me. It was reported that I died, or was missin', but I pulled through. I been trailin' you a long time. It's a long story——'

"I didn't wait to hear it. Went up to my room and sat down. After a while she come up. 'You see how 'tis,' she said. 'I've got to take care of him. Yer a good man, Jim; I admire yer spunk, a-askin' and a-askin', an never takin' 'no' fer an answer. As it is, if you care fer me I wisht you'd go,'

"I packed right up an' pulled out. No, I never did have no luck with women. Sence that happened I ain't had a chance to tackle another one."

Jim took great interest in Nät-ah'-ki and me. "My Gawd!" he would say, "just hear her laugh. She's sure happy. I wisht I had such a nice woman."

He spent much time in the trade room, and went often through the camp seeking to make a conquest of some fair damsel. He was really ridiculous, smiling at them, bowing and saying something in English which none could understand. The maidens turned away from him abashed. The men looking on either scowled or laughed and joked and named him the One-unable-to-marry, a very bad name in Blackfoot.

The main trouble was that he wore an immense mustache and chin whiskers. The Blackfeet abhorred hair, except that of the head. An old acquaintance never buttoned his shirt winter nor summer; his chest was as hairy as a dog's back. I have seen the Blackfeet actually shudder when they looked at it. But a happy day was coming for Jim. On a trip out from Fort Benton, Berry brought him a letter containing great news. A woman back in Missouri whom he had known from childhood had consented to marry him. He left for the States at once by the way of Corinne. We heard from him several months later: "Dear friends," he wrote, "she died the day before I got here. I'm sure grievin'. They's a nuther one here, but she's got seven children, an' she's after me. I take the Santy Fé trail tomorrer. Hain't I sure out of luck?"

We had a good trade that winter, but troublous times followed. A part of the Piegans, the Bloods and Blackfeet became a real terror to the whites in the country, and it was really unsafe to try to trade outside of Fort Benton. We passed the following two winters there. In January of the second one the Baker massacre occurred, and the Indians at once quieted down. In the spring of 1870 we began to plan for another season.

CHAPTER 20

The Ways of the Northland

A LAW prohibiting the sale of liquor to Indians, or its transportation across the Indian country, had been practically a dead letter ever since Congress passed it. Along in the fall of 1869, however, a new United States marshal appeared in the country and arrested several traders who had liquor in their possession, confiscated their outfits, and made them all sorts of trouble. So long as this man remained in office it seemed as if the trade was doomed, and Berry wisely hit upon the plan of crossing the line into Canada and establishing a post there. True, there would be some trouble in transporting the forbidden goods from Fort Benton northward to the line, but chances had to be taken.

Miss Agnes E. Laut, author of *Lords of the North, Heralds of the Empire,* etc., in her *Tales of the Northwest Mounted Police* has this to say about the exodus:

It was in the early seventies that the monopoly of the Hudson's Bay Company ceased and the Dominion Government took

over judicial rights in all that vast territory which lies like an
American Russia between the boundary and the North Pole.
The ending of the monopoly was the signal of an inrush of adventurers. Gamblers, smugglers, criminals of every stripe,
struck across from the Missouri into the Canadian territory at
the foothills of the Rockies. Without a white population, these
riff-raff adventurers could not ply their usual wide-open traffic.
The only way to wealth was by the fur trade; and the easiest
way to obtain the furs was by smuggling whisky into the country
in small quantities, diluting this and trading it to the natives
for pelts. Chances of interference were nil, for the Canadian
Government was thousands of miles distant without either tele-
graph or railway connection. But the game was not without its
dangers. The country at the foothills was inhabited by the Confederacy of the Blackfeet—Bloods, Piegans and Blackfeet—tigers of the prairie when sober, and worse than tigers when
drunk. The Missouri whisky smugglers found they must either
organise for defence or pay for their fun by being exterminated.
How many whites were massacred in these drinking frays will
never be known; but all around Old Man's River and Fort Macleod are gruesome landmarks known as the places where such
and such parties were destroyed in the early seventies.

The upshot was that the Missouri smugglers emulated the
old fur traders and built themselves permanent forts; Robbers'
Roost, Stand Off, Freeze Out, and most famous of all, Whoop-
Her-Up, whose name for respectability's sake has been changed
to "Whoop-Pup," with an innocent suggestiveness of some poetic
Indian title. Whoop-Up, as it was known to plainsmen, was
palisaded and loopholed for musketry, with bastions and cannon
and an alarm bell. The fortifications of this place alone, it is
said, cost $12,000, and it at once became the metropolis of the
whisky smugglers. Henceforth only a few Indians were allowed
inside the fort at a time, the rest being served through the
loopholes.

But the Blackfeet, who loved a man hunt better than a buffalo
hunt, were not to be balked. The trail by which the whisky
smugglers came from Fort Benton zigzagged over the rolling
prairie, mainly following the bottoms of the precipitous coulées
and ravines for a distance of 200 miles to Whoop-Up. Heavy

wagons with canvas tops and yokes of fifteen and twenty oxen
drew the freight of liquor through the devious passes that connected ravine with ravine. The Blackfeet are probably the best
horsemen in the world. There were places where the defiles were
exceptionally narrow, where the wagons got mired, where oxen
and freight had to be rafted across rain-swollen sloughs. With
a yelling of incarnate fiends that would have stampeded more
sober brutes than oxen drawing kegs of whisky, down swooped
the Blackfeet at just these hard spots. Sometimes the raids took
place at night, when tethers would be cut and the oxen
stampeded with the bellowing of a frightened buffalo herd. If
the smugglers made a stand there was a fight. If they drew off,
the savages captured the booty.

Miss Laut's informants have most grievously imposed upon
her. The men who participated in the trade across the line were
not "criminals of every stripe," but honest, fearless, straight-
forward fellows. Very many of them have been wronged by
Miss Laut's statements. Neither were they smugglers into the
country, for that part of Canada was then to the Canadians an
unknown land, without any laws or white residents. Away up
on the Saskatchewan was the Hudson's Bay Company selling
rum to the Indians, as they had been doing for many years. In
the opposition of the Americans they saw the end of their lu-
crative trade, and complained to the Dominion Government
about it, finally getting relief with the appearance of the Northwest Mounted Police. Neither were there any drinking frays
in which whites were massacred. One man named Joe Neufrain
was killed for cause by the Blackfeet at Elbow, about 100 miles
north of Belly River. Two men, a Frenchman named Polite,
and Joseph Wey, were killed at Rocky Springs, on the trail
from Fort Benton north. The Assiniboins, not the Blackfeet,
shot them. The fact is that the trail did not follow precipitous
coulées and ravines but ran straight over the open rolling plain,
the freighters thereon were not attacked by the Blackfeet, and
their cattle stampeded. Nor did they freight whisky in heavy
loaded bull trains. In crossing the Indian country south of the

line they had the United States marshal to elude; the whisky
was transported by four-horse teams which traveled swiftly
across by a route which the marshal was unlikely to know.

In the fall of 1870 Berry established Stand-Off; after that
Whoop-Up and Fort Kipp were built. There were one or two
other minor posts at Elbow, on High River, and Sheep Creek.
In all, from 1870 until the arrival of the Mounted Police in
1874, there were fifty-six white men at these various places or
camped out on the plains wolfing. They were not massacred by
the Blackfeet. When the Mounted Police came they also got
along peaceably with the Confederacy.

Starting north from Fort Benton with a good outfit of stores,
Berry, I, and several others arrived at Belly River, some
twenty-five or thirty miles above its mouth, and built Stand-
Off, a place of a few rude cabins. This is why we gave it the
peculiar name: The marshal got on our trail and overtook us
soon after we had crossed the North Fork of Milk River and
were descending the slope to the St. Mary's.

"Well, boys," he said, smiling grimly, "I've caught you at
last. Turn around and hit the back trail with me."

"I don't think we will," said Berry. "We're across the line.
Better turn around and go back yourself."

A warm argument ensued. The line had never been surveyed, but we knew that according to the treaty it was the 49th
parallel. We were on the Arctic Slope watershed, and therefore
we assumed that we were in Canada; the marshal said that we
were not. Finally Berry told him that he would not turn back,
that he would fight first, as he knew that he was right. The
marshal was powerless to take us, as he was alone. We "stood
him off," and he sorrowfully turned back.

Another time Berry went into Fort Benton for liquor and
the marshal trailed him around day and night. Nothing was
to be done there, so he hitched up his four-horse team and with
another man traveled up to Helena. Still the marshal followed,
but Berry was a man of resource. He went to a certain firm

there and got them to deliver thirty cases of alcohol to him on the banks of the Missouri a few miles below town, where he made a raft for the cargo, got aboard, and pushed out into the current. Meanwhile the marshal was watching the four horses and wagon at the livery stable. That night Berry's helper got them out and started on the back trail. In a little while the officer caught up with the outfit, but the wagon was empty and Berry was missing. He turned back and stayed all that night in Helena, then started again and arrived in Fort Benton about the same time as did the team. There the man loaded up with straight provisions and pulled out for the north. The marshal was completely nonplussed.

Meanwhile Berry was having a hard time. A raft of alcohol proved a difficult thing to handle, and in rapid water was sometimes completely submerged. Sometimes it stuck on a bar or was in danger of hitting a rocky shore and he had to jump off and push it into deeper water. For three days he played beaver, and practically fasted, for his provisions got wet, but on the third evening he reached the mouth of Sun River with the loss of but one case of alcohol, which the rocks had punctured. There a four-horse team awaited him, sent from Fort Benton by the driver of his own outfit. The two men at once loaded up the wagon and struck out over the trackless prairie, crossing the line and arriving at Stand-Off without trouble.

The Bloods and Blackfeet gave us a fair trade that winter. We realized, however, that with the building of Whoop-Up we were too far west to be in the center of the trade; so the succeeding summer we moved down some miles and built another post. The main event of the succeeding winter was the killing of Calf Shirt, the Blood chief. He was absolutely ferocious and his people feared him, having killed six or eight of them— several his own relatives. He came into the trade room one day and pointing a pistol at the man on duty there, demanded whisky. The trader raised his pistol and fired, the bullet taking effect in the Indian's breast. He did not drop, however, or even stagger; nor did he shoot, but turned and walked calmly out of the door toward his camp. Upon hearing the shot a number of men elsewhere in the post rushed out, saw the pistol in his hand, and thinking that he had killed someone, began firing. Shot after shot struck Calf Shirt, but he kept walking calmly on for many yards, and then fell over dead. He possessed extraordinary vitality. The body was thrown into the river through a hole in the ice, but it came up in an airhole below, and was found there. The chief had always told his wives that if he was killed they were to sing certain songs over his body, and he would come to life, if they kept it up for four days. The women took the corpse home and did as they had been told, and felt very badly when they found that their efforts were fruitless. All the rest of the tribe, however, rejoiced that the terror was gone.

Many of the traders had thousands of dollars worth of merchandise in stock when the Mounted Police drew near, and most of them were warned in time of their approach to bury, or otherwise conceal the liquor. A band of hunters brought the news. "Some men are coming," they said, "who wear red coats, and they are drawing a cannon."

That was sufficient for Berry and me, and we promptly cached the ten or twelve gallons of whisky we had. Only one trader, I believe, failed to get the warning; he had his whole stock confiscated because among it were found a few gallons of liquor. Of course, we were not glad to see the strangers, but we met them with courtesy and treated them well. Although they had come through a country teeming with game they were in an almost starving condition, and were very glad to buy our provisions. Their commander, Colonel Macleod, was a gentleman, and became a life-long friend with some of the "smugglers." Many of the traders remained in that country to continue trade with the Indians and the newcomers, while others returned to Montana. We went with the latter outfits.

Thus passed the trade in the north. I cannot say that we regretted it. Prices of furs had fluctuated and dropped in value 100 per cent, few had cleared anything worth mentioning. Four years later the last of the Alberta buffalo herds drifted south and never returned to that section of the country.

We again took up our quarters in Fort Benton at the little adobe house and wintered there. It was a relief to be out of the trade for a time and rest up. A few of those who had been in the north with us crossed the river and located ranches on the Shonkin and along the Highwood Mountains.

CHAPTER 21

The Story of Ancient Sleeper

AS the days passed, Berry fidgeted around and was cross, and I became nervous and edgy, too. "My father always told me," he said one day, "that a man who stayed in the fur trade was a fool. One might make a stake one winter, but he would be sure to lose it another season. He was right. Let's give it up, buy some cattle with what we have left, and settle down to stock raising."

"All right," I agreed. "Anything suits me."

"We'll do some ploughing," he went on, "and raise potatoes and oats and all kinds of garden stuff. I tell you, it'll be fine."

Berry's bull train had just pulled in from a trip to Helena. We loaded it with some lumber, doors and windows, what furniture we had, plenty of provisions and some tools, hired a couple of good axe-men, and started it out, going on ahead with the women with a four-horse team. We chose a location on Back Fat Creek, not far from the foot of the Rockies, and less than one hundred miles from Fort Benton. We selected a site for the buildings, and then, leaving me to superintend their erection,

Berry went away with a couple of men to purchase some cattle. It did not take long to haul enough pine logs from the mountains for a six-room shack, a stable and corral, and by the time Berry returned with the cattle, about four hundred head, I had everything fixed for winter, even enough hay for a team and a couple of saddle horses.

We had some trouble with the cattle at first, but in a few weeks they located, and thereafter it required little riding to keep them close herded. I can't say that I did much of the riding, but Berry enjoyed it. We had a couple of men, so I went out on little hunts with Nät-ah'-ki, poisoned wolves, caught trout in the deep holes of the creek, and just stayed home.

The room Nat-ah'-ki and I occupied had a rude stove and mud fireplace, as did all the others except the kitchen, where was a good big stove. Previous to this, except when in Fort Benton, the women had always used a fireplace for cooking, and they still used one for roasting meat, and baking beans in a Dutch oven. Besides a bed and a chair or two, our room had a bureau of which Nät-ah'-ki was very proud. She was always washing and dusting it, although it was never in need of such care, and arranging and re-arranging the contents of the drawers. Also, we had curtains to the window, tied back with blue ribbons, and there was a table which I made of a dry goods box, covered with a bright blanket. At one side of the fireplace was a buffalo robe couch, willow backrests at each end. We had some argument over that. When I explained what I wanted, Nät-ah'-ki objected to its construction. "You disappoint me," she complained. "Here we have built a home, and furnished it with beautiful things—" pointing to the bureau, bed, and curtains—"and we are living like white people, trying to be white, and now you want to spoil it all by fixing up an Indian couch!" But of course I had my way.

One evening we visited a camp of some thirty lodges, of which one, Ancient Sleeper, was the head man. He owned a medicine pipe and various other sacred things, and did some doctoring, in which, besides various concoctions of herbs that

were given the patient internally or externally, a mountain-
lion skin, and prayers to that animal, played an important
part. When we entered his lodge, I was welcomed and motioned
to a place on his left, Nät-ah'-ki of course taking her seat near
the doorway with the women. Above the old man, securely tied
to the lodge poles, hung his medicine pipe, bound in many
wrappings of various skins. Spread over the backrest at the
right end of his couch was the sacred lion skin. In front of him
his everyday pipe of black stone rested upon a large buffalo
chip. Long before, I had heard, his dream had commanded this,
and ever since the pipe he smoked had never been laid on the
ground. As in the lodges of other medicine men, no one was
permitted to walk entirely around the fire, thus passing between it and the medicines, nor could any one remove fire from
the lodge, for by so doing the power of his medicine might be
broken.

Ancient Sleeper mixed tobacco and l'herbe, chopping it fine,
filled his pipe, passed it to me to light, and we smoked together
by turns. When I received the pipe, I took it from him with one
hand; when I passed it to him, he grasped the stem with both
hands, palms down, spreading and crooking his fingers, seizing,
pouncing upon it, in imitation of the way of a bear. Thus did
all medicine-pipe men; it was a sign of their order. We talked
a little—about the weather, the game, the whereabouts of the
people. The women set before us some food, and I ate of it as
in dutybound. I had gone to the lodge with a purpose, and I
began to edge around to it. I told him I had at various times
in various places killed mountain lions. "I see you have the
skin of one there," I concluded. "Did you kill it, or was it a
present?"

"The Sun was good to me," he replied. "I killed it. It was all
ik-ut'-o-wap-i (very sun power; very—let us translate it—su-
pernatural) that which occurred.

"I was a man. I had a lodge of my own, my three women
whom you see here. My body was strong. I was successful in
everything. I was happy. And then all this changed. If I went

to war, I got wounded. If I took horses, I lost them again; they died, or were stolen, or crippled themselves. Although I hunted hard, somehow I often failed to bring home meat.

"And then came the worst of all, sickness. Some bad ghost or evil thing got inside of me, and at times would grip my heart, so that the pain was terrible. When it did that, no matter where I was, what I was doing, the pain was so great that I became dizzy and staggered, and sometimes I just fell over and died for a short time. I doctored; I had the medicine men pray for me, giving a horse here, a horse there. I did not get any better, and I became very poor. At last we had only enough horses with which to move camp. Parties would no longer allow me to go to war with them. They feared that I would die on their hands, or in some way bring misfortune.

I heard of a man, a Gros Ventre, who had suffered with the same trouble. He had bought a medicine pipe of great power, and by its use he had got well. He would sell the pipe, I was told, but I could not buy it. I had no fifteen or twenty horses to give for it nor even one. I preferred to die rather than have my women go afoot. Neither had I relatives to help me nor had my women any who could do so. I was very poor. Still somehow, I kept up courage, trying in every way to get well, and to provide for myself and mine. At last my dying times became so frequent that I no longer went hunting or anywhere, except when one of my women accompanied me. They would not let me go off by myself.

"She there, my last woman, went with me one day on a hunt. We were camping at the time on the Pi-is-tum-is-i-sak-ta (Deep Creek) away up toward the headwaters, and we went on foot up into the pines of the Belt Mountains in search of anything that was meat. We traveled far before we found much fresh sign. At last, away up high on the mountain side I saw a band of elk move across an opening and disappear in the timber which surrounded it. The wind was right and I followed them, my woman keeping close behind me.

"Down into a deep coulée they went, across the stream at

the bottom of it, and up the other side. But when we came to
the stream we stopped, for there in the trail, fresh on top of
the hoof marks of the elk, were the footprints of a grizzly bear,
a very large one. He, too, was hunting, and he was before me
on the trail of the elk. I gave it to him and turned back. I did
not wish to meet him there among the thick pines. We came
again to the opening and went into the timber in another direction, up toward the summit of the mountain. We found more
fresh elk sign and followed it very cautiously step by step,
looking, looking everywhere for sight of the animals.

"At last we came to the foot of a high cliff. Under it were
broken rocks, bushes, low pines. Right out where the sun shone
on it full, lay an elk, a two-year-old bull, head bent around to
its side, fast asleep. I had but my bow and arrows. To make a
sure shot, I must get close either above or below it for the
animal lay lengthwise with the cliff, and I had approached it
from behind. I chose to go along the foot of the cliff, and shoot
downward. Never did I step more carefully, more slowly. I had
to get that elk, for we were without meat, had lived for some
days on that given us by more successful hunters. My woman
had stopped and sat down to give me more chance in the approach. I glanced back and saw her looking at me, at the elk,
signing me to be cautious. I went even more carefully, if that
were possible, and was at last in a good position to shoot. I
drew back the bow and let go the string. I saw the arrow sink
down into the elk, saw it struggle to rise, saw blood stream
from its nostrils, and then the pain gripped my heart. I staggered and died.

"I was a very long time dead, for when I came to life the sun
had set and the last of his colors were fading behind him. I was
lying in a sort of cave where my woman had carried me. I felt
too weak to get up. She brought plenty of wood and made a
little fire at the mouth of the cave. Then she brought water in
a piece of the elk skin, and some meat. I drank, and she fed me
some roast liver, a marrow bone, a kidney, but I was not hungry; I could eat only a few mouthfuls. Nor could she eat. We
felt very sad. Each of us knew that this time I had almost really

died. She came and lay down beside me and smoothed my forehead, speaking words of courage, and after a little time I fell asleep.

"Then my shadow went forth from my worn body. I was free, as light as the bubble of the stream. I felt able to travel wherever I wished to, and to understand all things. Thus, as if I had been led, or shown the way, I came to a fine, new, big lodge standing all by itself at the edge of a grove, in a deep, wide valley in which was a beautiful stream. Without hesitating, without bashfulness, I raised the door skin and entered the lodge. An old, old man was its owner, and he welcomed me, gave me a seat beside him, told his woman to prepare food. We smoked, and he asked many questions. I told him the story of my life, how I now suffered. 'Yes' he kept saying, and 'yes,' and 'Yes.' 'I know—I understand.'

"We ate that which the woman set before us, and he again filled the pipe. 'Listen,' he said, as we smoked. 'Listen. Once I suffered as you do, and, like you, I sought everywhere, in many ways for help, and at last it was given to me. I regained my health. My hair has turned white, my skin wrinkles, I am very, very old; yet still my body is strong and sound, and I myself provide the meat for this lodge. All this because I found a powerful helper. I pity you. As I was told to do, I will now tell you; heed my words and follow the advice, and you, too, will live to great age.

"'Some ghost, perhaps that of an enemy you have killed, has in some way entered your body and set up an evil growth in your stomach. It must be removed for it grows larger and larger, pressing against the heart, and unless it is checked, will soon press so hard that the heart cannot work—then death. You must kill a mountain lion, have the skin tanned, leaving the claws on the feet. You must take good care of this skin, and at night hang it or place it near the head of your couch. So, when you lie down to sleep you will pray, saying, 'Hai'-yu! maker of claws; Hai'-yu! maker of sharp, cutting claws, I pray you to aid me; claw away this thing which is threatening my life, and will surely kill me without your aid!' Thus you must pray to

the maker of claws, to the shadow of the ancient lion himself.
Also, you must learn these songs—and he taught me three.
Ancient Person sang them, needless to say, with all the deep,
sincere feeling that the devout express in their sacred songs.
Also, he said, I must always lay my pipe on a buffalo chip, for
the buffalo was a sacred animal, and that when I prayed, blowing smoke to the four directions of the world, to those above,
and to our mother (earth) my prayers would have more power.

"It must have been far away where I found that good old
man, for my shadow did not return to my body until after
sunrise. I awoke and saw it shining into the cave. My woman
had rebuilt the fire, was cooking. 'Let that be for a time,' I said,
'and come and sit with me.' I told her all, where I had been,
what the kind old man had said, and she was glad. Right there
one-half of the arrows in my quiver, with the tongue of the elk
I had killed, we hung up as a sacrifice, and then we went home,
my woman carrying meat, as much as was possible for her to
handle. I could carry but little.

"I had a North gun (Hudson's Bay Company's make), but no
powder and no balls. The one flint was bad. From a friend I
borrowed a trap and in a short time I caught six beavers with
it. Another friend going in to Fort Benton to trade took them
with him and brought me what I needed, new flints and ammunition, and then I began to hunt mountain lions. I had never
hunted mountain lions, nor had any of our people. Some one
occasionally came across one and killed it, and he was thought
to be a lucky man, for the skins of these animals have always
been medicine. They are made into quiver and bow cases, or
the owners use them for saddle skins. Used in any way, they
give one success in hunting or in war. Again my wife and I
went afoot into the mountains. I took both gun and bow, the
latter for killing meat. The silent arrow alarms nothing. The
boom of a gun arouses every living thing; the sleeping ones
awake, prick up their ears, sniff the wind and watch.

"We walked along the shore of the creek. Here, there, plainly
marked in the mud, and on damp sand were footprints of those
I sought, footprints, but nothing more. We went into the deep

timber. Although many might have passed there, they could make no sign, leave no tracks on the dry, dead leaves. We went higher, up through the timber, up where the rock is chief and trees grow small and low. There we sat all through the day, peering out through bushes surrounding the place, seeing once a small black bear, once a fisher, but no other living thing, except little birds, and eagles lazily flying around. But near sunset came a band of bighorn feeding toward us, following the wind. I fitted an arrow to my bow and shot one, a little young one. It bleated and fell over. I then shot the mother. We left her lying, in hopes of finding a mountain lion by it the next day, and taking the young one we went away down the mountain and camped for the night near a stream of water.

"We passed many days like that, many days. We camped wherever night came upon us, going home only when our lodge required meat, or when camp was to be moved. Thus passed the summer, and in all that time we saw not once that which I sought. Twice during that time I died, and each time I was dead longer than before. I became much discouraged. I did not doubt my dream's words, but I felt that I was going to die before I could do all the old man had told me to do.

"Then came winter, and snow fell on the high slopes, falling lower, still lower, until the mountains were white clear to the plains. Nothing was now hidden from me of the happenings of the night. Wherever I went the snow gave me the story as well as if some one had looked on, had seen it all, and then related it. Here walked, and fed, and played, and rested deer and elk; here a bear prowled around, turning over logs and stones. There were tracks of wolf, and coyote, and bobcat and fox, each hunting in his own way for something with which to fill his belly. Over there is a trail of big, round footprints near together. Here in the night a mountain lion sprang upon a buck deer, killed it and ate his fill, dragged the remains over to his place and covered them with all the loose things he could paw together. Thus I explained it to my woman. 'And,' I told her, 'he has not gone far; his belly is full. Somewhere near he lies stretched out, asleep.'

"I would trail him. I would go as carefully as he himself when he crept along, preparing to spring upon a deer. I would see him before he should awake and notice me, and I would kill him where he lay. I was excited. After all these moons at last I had a trail to follow, and on the snow that was almost as good as seeing the animal far off and approaching him. Think then, friend, think of my despair when, almost within sight of the covered deer, I found where the animal had lain on a big log, and seen us talking, and bounded away into the dark woods with long leaps! It was too much. Again I got dizzy, staggered, and was dead before I dropped upon the snow.

"That time my woman got me home, going back for a horse for me to ride, and I lay in the lodge many days, weak in body, sick in heart, discouraged. But friends came in to cheer me. Their women brought choice meat, and tongues, dried berries, soups, anything good. So we fared well, and day by day my strength came back. At last, one evening, a friend who had been hunting came hurrying in. 'Kyi!' said he, 'I have good news for you. Up in a cañon where I trailed a wounded deer, I came to a hole in the rocks. A hard-beaten trail leads from it out to the water, then parts into many smaller trails. A mountain lion lives there with her young. I did not scare them. I did not even kill the deer I followed to the place, but came at once to tell you.'

"Once more I took courage, and as soon as it was daylight I started for the place with my friend and my woman. We rode away to the south, then up a creek, tied our horses and entered a walled cañon. From there it was not far to the cave. Snow had fallen during the night and the freshest tracks led into the cave. In there was the mother, and three young, partly grown, and they were somewhere back in the darkness, watching us perhaps.

"I was frightened. Of course I was. Men had been killed by these animals when following them into their dens. And this one had young; she would fight all the more fiercely. Yes, I was afraid, but for all that I must go in, as well die there as in some other place, of the sickness from which I suffered. My woman cried and begged me not to go. My friend proposed that we sit and watch for the animals to come out, but I fixed the priming in my gun, took my knife in my teeth, got down on my hands and knees and crawled into the cave. It was just a narrow, low hole in the wall, and my body shut off most of the light, yet there was enough for me to see ahead dimly, and after a little I saw before me two green-red eyes, big, wide eyes of fire. I stooped lower, letting in more light, and could see the old one's body, see her ears laid back tight on her head, see the tip of her tail swishing this way, that way. She growled a little, a low, soft growl. She lay on her belly and her forefeet shifted back and forth, seeking the secure hold. She was about to spring. I slowly raised my gun, but before I could aim it, she sprang. I fired. The ball met her in the air, her body struck me and knocked the breath out of me, and once more I died.

"They pulled me out of the cave, and, while my woman cared for me, my friend went back in, shot the three young with his bow and arrows, and dragged them out with the body of the mother. My ball had struck her fair in the breast. So, now, at last, I had that which my dream had told me to get, and I prayed, I sang the songs as I had been told to do. It was not many nights after that, sitting on my couch, I said the prayers and sang the first of the songs. I had just finished it when something gave way inside of me, and blood and foul matter streamed from my mouth. There was no pain. After a time the blood ceased running. I washed my mouth, got up and walked around. I no longer felt a tightness in my side. I felt light on foot, as if I could run and jump, and I was hungry. I knew what had happened; even as the old man had foretold, the growth inside of me had been clawed open. I was well. We made great sacrifice for this next day. I have been well ever since. Not only that, but my medicine has cured many sick ones. Kyi!"

This was a happy winter. It was for all of us except Berry, who chafed over the endless days of cold and snow. I don't know how many times he went down on the flat and measured it. So many acres here for oats, so many there for potatoes, for turnips, for peas. We would buy a lot of sows, he said, and raise pigs as well as cattle. Spring came early. Toward the end of March the bulls were rounded up and yoked to the plows. Old Mrs. Berry and the Crow Woman prepared a little plot of ground in a bend of the creek, and sorted seeds they had obtained at some distant time from their people, the Mandans and Rees. I didn't know anything about ploughing and planting, nor did I wish to learn.

Nät-ah'-ki and I rode among the cattle—and found that the calves disappeared about as fast as they were born. Wolves were numerous.

In June more than a foot of snow fell upon our fields of growing things, and when it melted, there came a frost and froze everything. Berry cursed loud and frequently. In July and August we tried to put up some hay, but rain spoiled it as fast as it was cut. In the fall we had no grain to thresh, no potatoes nor turnips, not even cabbage to put into our big root house. After the fall branding, we found that we had an increase in our cattle of only fifteen per cent. The wolves were accountable for the additional forty-five per cent we should have had. "This ranching and cattle raising," said Berry, "isn't what it's cracked up to be. Let's sell out and get back into the trade. There's more fun and excitement in that anyhow."

Of course I agreed to that, and he went into Fort Benton to find a buyer for the place. He found one, but the man would not make the deal until spring, so we put in another winter there, which was also a happy one to some of us—for Nät-ah'-ki and me, at least.

May found us again installed in the little abode in Fort Benton, but not for long. Berry was anxious to be doing something and, learning that Fort Conrad was for sale, we bought it. This place was built at the upper end of a large bottom on the Marias River, where the Dry Fork joins the larger stream. It was not much of a fort, just two rows of connecting log cabins, with stables and a corral at the west end of them, the whole thing forming three sides of a square. It was a good location, however, for, besides the trade in robes we expected to get, it was on the trail between Fort Benton and Fort Macleod, and the travel and freighting over it was heavy in the summer time. The women were especially pleased with the purchase. They had regretted leaving our home on Back Fat Creek, but now they had another one, farther away from the mountains, where the summers were warmer and longer. "Here," said Crow Woman, "my beans and corn and squash will surely grow. I am glad."

"This is happiness," Nät-ah'-ki said, as we sat in the shade of a big cottonwood by the river's edge. "See the beautiful trees above there, and below, and the pretty island with its young timber. And on all sides the high, steep hills—protection from the winter winds."

"Yes," I said, "it is a pretty place. I like it better than I did the other one."

"Say this for me," she continued, leaning over and drawing me to her. "Say this: we will live here always; live here until we die, and they bury us out across there where the big trees grow."

I said it, and added thereto, "If it be possible for us to do so," watching the expectant, pleased expression of her eyes suddenly change to one of pain.

"Oh, why," she asked, "why did you spoil it all? Don't you know that you can do anything you wish to?"

"No, I don't," I replied. "No one can always do what he wishes to do. But let us not worry; we will try to live here always."

"Yes," she sighed, "we will try; we will have courage. Oh, good Sun, kind Sun! Pity us! Let us live here in peace and happiness to great age."

Even then Berry and I had some idea of the changes that were to take place, but we did not dream that they were so near at hand. We looked for the old, free, careless times to last for fifteen or twenty years at least.

CHAPTER 22

A Game of Fate

DURING the summer we had put in a good stock of merchandise, expecting to have a fine winter trade at the fort, but now came the disquieting news that there were practically no buffalo to the north, the west, or the south of us. We could not believe it at first; it seemed impossible; but the great herds had drifted southeastward from the plains of northwestern Canada into Montana, and they never recrossed the line. This was the winter of 1878–79. South of the Missouri to the Yellowstone and beyond, the buffalo were, however, apparently as plentiful as ever.

The Piegans had intended to winter in the vicinity of Fort Conrad and trade with us, but of course they were obliged to change their plans and go to buffalo, and we had to accompany them to get any trade at all. We left it to the women whether they would remain at home or accompany us, and all but Nätah'-ki elected to stay at the fort. Her prompt decision to accompany me was exceedingly pleasing, for I had felt that it would be well-nigh impossible to go alone, even for a few months.

We pulled out, Berry, Nät-ah'-ki and I, with a couple of four-horse team loads, leaving a man to look after the fort and the women. Traveling by way of Fort Benton, we were several days passing the mouth of the Marias. Just beyond that point the sight of buffalo on all sides gladdened our eyes, and we found the Piegan camp, pitched at the foot of the Bear Paws, red with meat, littered with drying hides. Nät-ah'-ki's mother was on hand as soon as we came to a stop, and the two women put up our lodge while Berry and I unharnessed and cared for our stock. We finally turned them over to a boy who was to herd for us.

Big Lake's shadow had some time since departed for the Sandhills. White Calf was now the head chief of the tribe, and after him, Running Crane, Fast Buffalo Horse, and Three Suns were the principal men. They were big-hearted, brave, kindly men, ever ready to help the distressed by word and deed. Our lodge was no sooner set up and supper under way than they came in to smoke and feast with us, Nät-ah'-ki's mother having gone around to invite them. Also came Weasel Tail and Talks-with-the-buffalo and Bear Head and other friends. The talk was mainly about the disappearance of the buffalo. Some thought that they might have crossed the mountains; that the Nez Percés or some other tribe of the other side had found some means to drive or decoy them to the plains of the Columbia. Old Red Eagle, the great medicine-pipe man, declared that his dream had reliably informed him about the matter: "As it happened before in the long ago," he said, "so it is now. Some evil one has driven them into a great cave or natural corral in the mountains, and there holds them in his hate of us to whom they belong. They must be found and released, their captor killed. Were it not that I am blind, I would undertake to do it myself. Yes, I would start tomorrow and keep on, until I found them."

"Have patience; in summer our young men will go out to war, and they will search for the missing herds."

"Ai! Ai!" the old man grumbled. "Have patience! That is what they always say. It wasn't so in my day; was there something to do, we did it; now it is put off for fear of winter's cold or summer's heat."

White Calf closed the subject by saying that even if some one had cached the northern herds, there seemed to be a plenty left. "And they're on our own land, too," he added. "If any of the other-side people come over here to hunt, we'll see that they never return."

The feast over, and our guests departed, people began to flock in to trade. One for a rifle; another for cartridges; others for tobacco, or sugar, coffee, and some for spirits. We had nearly a wagonload of alcohol, which we diluted, four to one, as occasion required. Before bedtime we sold over five hundred dollars' worth of goods, wet and dry, and it was easy to see that Berry would be kept pretty constantly on the road all winter, hauling our furs to Fort Benton and returning with fresh supplies of merchandise.

There was an unusual craze for gambling that winter. At night the camp resounded with the solemn, weird, gambling chant from many lodges. There the players sat, the two sides facing each other, and played the "hide the bone game," striking with small sticks the outer rail of the couches in time to the song. Even the women gambled, and many were the altercations over their bets.

In a lodge near us lived a young couple, Fisher and his woman, The Lark. They were devoted to each other, and were always together, even on the hunts. People smiled, pleased to see the untiring love they had for each other. Fisher was a fine hunter and kept his lodge well supplied with meats and skins, and he was a successful warrior, too, as his large herd of horses testified. But sometimes, when The Lark was chipping a robe, Fisher strolled to the nearest game and played for a while. He was quite expert at it and frequently won more than he lost.

But one evil day he played against young Glancing Arrow, and lost ten head of horses. I got news of the game, and listened to the comments on it. Glancing Arrow, it seemed, had himself wanted to set up a lodge with The Lark. Although he was a rich young man her parents had rejected his horses and given her to the Fisher, who was not nearly so well off. This had pleased every one, for the Fisher was loved by every one, while Glancing Arrow was surly, cross-grained, miserly and had not a single close friend. He had been heard to say that he would yet have The Lark for his woman.

"Fisher is crazy to gamble with him," said one of my customers. "To gamble with the best player in the camp, and the man who is his enemy."

Sore over his loss, the Fisher sought out Glancing Arrow, played the bone game with him nearly all night, and lost twelve more horses. In the forenoon The Lark came over to visit Nät-ah'-ki, and I was called into the conference. The woman was crying and sorely distressed. "He is sleeping now," she said, "but when he awakes he is going to play with Glancing Arrow again. I have begged him not to, but for the first time he refuses to listen to me. Just think, twenty-two horses are already lost, nearly half of our band, and to that dog, Glancing Arrow!

"Go over and talk with him," she continued. "He will listen to you. Go and talk him out of this madness."

I walked over to their lodge and found the Fisher still in bed, lying propped up on one arm and staring moodily at the fire. "You needn't say it," he began, before I could open my mouth. "I know why you have come. She sent you to ask me to play no more, but I'm not going to stop. I can't stop until I have won back all that I have lost."

"But look here," I put in. "You may lose more if you keep on, perhaps all you have, for I hear Glancing Arrow is the most skillful of all the players. Just think how much you are risking, what a shame it would be were you to be set afoot, no horses with which to move camp, not even one for your woman to ride."

"Oh! that could not happen," he said confidently. "I could not lose them all. No, there is no use of your talking. I must play again with him, and I'm sure that I will win. I shall pray. I shall make a sacrifice. I must win."

The sun had not long set before the Fisher and Glancing Arrow met in the lodge of Heavy Top. A big crowd gathered

to encourage the Fisher. The Lark came over to our lodge and
sat with Nät-ah'-ki, who tried to cheer her and divert her
thoughts from her trouble. But she kept saying that she felt
something dreadful was going to happen. Time and again she
went out and stood by the lodge in which the gambling was
going on, listening and returning to tell us how the game progressed. "He has lost another horse," she would say; "they are
going one by one." Once she reported that the Fisher had won
one back. "But he'll lose it in the next game," she concluded
despondently and began to cry.

"Go over there," Nät-ah'-ki entreated me. "Do something,
say something to end it."

I went, sure that I was setting out on a useless errand. The
lodge was crowded, but I found a seat near the players. When
the Fisher saw me, he frowned and shook his head. I felt powerless.

By the side of Glancing Arrow lay a little heap of small, red-
painted sticks, used for markers, and each one represented a
horse, I looked over in front of his opponent and counted seven
sticks. The Fisher had, then, but seven horses left. "We will
play for two head this time," he said and threw two sticks on
the ground between them. The other placed a like number
beside them, and the Fisher took the bones, one red-painted,
the other with black bands. They began the song, the onlookers
also joining in and beating time on the couch rail. Manipulating
the little bones, the Fisher deftly passed them from one hand
to the other, back and forth, back and forth, carried his hands
within the robe folded across his lap, while he changed them
there; then, at the conclusion of the song, he suddenly extended
both fists toward his adversary, looking him steadily in the
eyes. Raising his clenched right hand, forefinger extended,
Glancing Arrow slapped it down into the palm of his left hand,
the forefinger pointing at the left fist. The Fisher reluctantly
opened it and exposed to view the black-band bone. He had
lost, and had now only five horses. He picked up the markers,
counted and recounted them, divided them into parts of two

and three, twos and one, and then bunching them, said: "These
are the last. I will play you for the five head."

Glancing Arrow's little eyes sparkled. They were set close
together in his hatchet face, and his large nose was very thin,
and bowed owl-beak-like over his thin lips. He quickly laid out
his five markers, and picked up the bones. Again the song
began and he crossed his hands back and forth, up and down,
forefingers crookedly extended. He rubbed them together,
opened them and exposed the black-banded bone, now in one
palm, now in the other, changing it so quickly that the observer
was bewildered. The instant the song ceased Fisher pointed to
the player's right hand, and the losing bone was tossed to him
from it.

"Well," he said, "I have still a rifle, a lodge, a saddle, war-
clothes, blankets, and robes. I will bet them all against ten
head of horses."

Glancing Arrow agreed, laying out ten markers, and again
manipulating the bones as the song was renewed. And, as
usual, Glancing Arrow won, and laughed loudly. The Fisher
shivered as if from cold, drew his robe about him, preparing
to leave. "Come over tomorrow," he said, "and I will turn it all
over to you—the horses and everything else."

"Wait!" Glancing Arrow exclaimed, as he arose. "I will give
you the chance to get back everything you have lost; I will bet
everything I have won from you—against your woman!"

Every one clapped his hand to his mouth in surprise, and
there was exclamations, deep and heartfelt, of horror and dis-
approval. "The dog!" one said. "Knock him on the head!" cried
another. "Throw him out!" others exclaimed.

But Glancing Arrow did not heed them; he sat nonchalantly
bunching and counting his markers, the smile still on his lips.
The Fisher shivered again, arose and passed around to the
doorway. There he stopped and stood like one in a trance. I
arose, too, and went over to him. "Come home with me." I said.
"Come to my lodge, your woman awaits you there."

"Yes, go!" said others. "Go home with him."

But he shook my hand from his shoulder and quickly returned to his seat. "Begin!" he cried to his adversary. "We will play. We will play for her." And he added under his breath, "For her and one other thing."

Perhaps Glancing Arrow did not hear the latter part of the sentence, or, if he did, he made no sign. He picked up the bones and began to sing, but no one joined in, not even the Fisher, and looking at the rows of sullen, scowling faces staring at him, he faltered, but kept on with it in a manner to the end, and extended his closed hands before him.

There ensued a moment of tense silence. If wishes could have killed, Glancing Arrow had died where he sat. I myself felt an almost uncontrollable desire to bury my fingers in his throat and choke him to death. Some, indeed, half rose from their seats, and I saw several hands gripping knife handles.

The Fisher looked him steadily in the eyes so long and with such an agonizing expression, that the suspense became almost unbearable. Twice he raised his hand to denote his choice, and twice drew back. But at last he pointed to the left fist, and received the unmarked bone!

Some of the onlookers sprang up. There were cries of "Kill him! Kill him!" Knives were drawn. Heavy Top reached for his carbine. But the Fisher motioned them back to their places, and there was that in his expression, something so quiet, and ominous, and determined, that they obeyed him. "Come tomorrow," he told the winner, "and you shall have all that you have won."

"No," said Glancing Arrow, "not tomorrow. I will take the lodge and the robes and the blankets and the woman to-night, the horses tomorrow."

"Come then. It shall be as you say."

We let them pass out into the darkness. No one followed, nor spoke. We all felt that something was going to happen. But some of those who had been standing outside listening, did follow, and there were several witnesses of the end of it all. The Lark had been standing behind the lodge, had heard herself put up for the last stake; heard the demand of the winner, and then she had fled homeward. A little later went the Fisher, followed by the man who had broken him. They went inside, a man or two entering in behind them.

"There she is!" the Fisher exclaimed, pointing to the couch where the woman lay completely covered with a buffalo robe. "There she is," he continued, "but you shall never touch her. I am going to make a sacrifice of you here in her presence."

His words and the expression of his face so paralyzed Glancing Arrow that he did not try to defend himself, but sank to the ground, crying. "Have pity, pity me!" even before the Fisher sprang upon him and thrust a knife again and again deep into his neck.

We in the lodge heard the dying man's screams and rushed out, tearing the lodge skin loose from its pegs as we went. When I had reached the scene, it was all over. Glancing Arrow lay dead beside the fire and the Fisher stood over him looking down at his work, a pleased, childish expression on his face.

"Why, yes, of course," he said, dreamily, "I remember he wanted her. He has always wanted her, my woman. And I have killed him. See, little woman, he is dead, completely dead. You need fear no more to go to the river for water, or to the timber for fuel. Get up and see for yourself—he is surely dead."

But The Lark did not move, and, bending over, he drew back her covering, and gave a heart-rending, gasping cry. She, too, was dead. Covering herself with her robe, she had grasped a knife in both hands and pressed it straight down into her heart. Her hands still firmly held the hilt, and if ever a dead face expressed anguish and horror, hers did. The sight seemed to bring the Fisher to his senses—I was sure that he had been demented for several days. "It is my fault," he said. "My fault, my fault! But you shall not go alone."

And before any of us could interfere, he plunged the knife he still held into his own bosom, and fell over beside her, blood streaming from his mouth. We fled; there was nothing we could do.

Women came and prepared the bodies for burial, and in the morning they were taken away and lashed in their aerial sepulchres.

Then we move away from the place, eastward to the next little creek. There was no gambling thereafter for a very long time, the whole camp mourned the two young lives we missed. The Blackfoot language is exceedingly poor in words for cursing; but such as it contains we used often to execrate the memory of Glancing Arrow.

CHAPTER 23

Trade, Hunt and War Party

BERRY was almost constantly on the road, so I had few opportunities to do any hunting. There were days when I saw a band of buffalo loping swiftly over the distant plain pursued by the hunters, or when some friend came into our lodge and told of an exciting chase—I found camp life irksome at such times, and longed to be able to go and come as I pleased.

"Tomorrow you shall be trader," I said to Năt-ah'-ki one evening, "and I will go hunting. I am getting weak sitting here in the lodge day after day."

"You shall go," she said. "Why didn't you tell me long ago? I can trade as well as you can. I know just how much to give for everything. But I will *not* put my thumb in the cup when I measure out sugar or coffee or tea."

"The cup has no handle."

"But there are other cups of the very same size with handles. You and Berry ought to be ashamed of yourselves, to so cheat these poor people. Now, here is the one—" picking up a new tin one that Berry had just brought from the Fort. "This is the one I shall use. See, it has a strong handle and—" she turned it over and over, examining inside and outside. "Why, what a strangely made cup; it has two bottoms; it will hold only a little more than half as much as a real cup. Oh, what rascals you traders are!"

"Wait!" I exclaimed, "you do not understand. There is another trader in this camp. He gives four cups of sugar for a wolf skin; with this one we will give seven cupfuls of sugar, or four of coffee, or five of tea. The people will get just as much for a skin or robe as they did before, but the other trader has no false cup; he cannot give as many real cupfuls; we will drive him out of here and get all of the trade."

And that is what we did. Berry was the man to get trade; no one could successfully compete with him.

I went hunting in the morning. There were six of us, including Big Plume and his nephew, a very bright, handsome, likeable young man named Moccasin. There were eight or ten inches of snow on the ground and thick, low clouds drifting southward obscured the sun. Snow fell intermittently, at times so fast that we could not see objects a hundred yards away. We rode for four or five miles, then a lull in the storm disclosed a half dozen bands of buffalo not half a mile farther on and across a wide coulée. We sat very still on our horses until another flurry of snow blotted out the landscape, when we rode down a side coulée, and across the large one, and climbed the hill on the other side. When we topped the rise we were right in the herd, and then it was every man for himself. We were half-blinded by the stinging clouds of snow their sharp hoofs threw into our eyes. The muffled reports of my companions' rifles sounded far off, my own seemed more like the discharge of a toy pistol than anything else, yet before I had emptied the magazine I saw three different victims stop, and stagger, and fall, and I felt that I had killed my share of the game, and brought my horse to a stop. The others did even better than I, and we were several hours skinning our kill and preparing the meat for packing. The women would come for it the next day, and Big Plume was to have my share taken in for one of the hides and part of the meat.

It was all of two o'clock when we started homeward, after

tying to our saddles the tongues and other choice parts of the buffalo. The wind had veered to northwest and was blowing harder, driving the snow in clouds before it. We had not progressed more than a mile, shielding our faces with our hands or blankets, and trusting to our horses to find the back trail, when someone cried out: "A war party ahead! Look! See them run!"

And sure enough, there they were, a couple of hundred yards distant, five men running as fast as they could for the shelter of a nearby coulée. Moccasin was ahead of us and he put the whip to his horse as soon as he sighted them, regardless of his uncle's cries to wait. Long before we could overtake him he had charged after them, firing his carbine rapidly, and we saw one of them fall. They, too, fired at him, and we saw that they carried muzzle-loaders. He was now almost on top of the four fleeing men when the one who had fallen rose up as he was passing and discharged a pistol at him, and doubling over in the saddle he hung on for a moment, then fell limply to the ground, his horse turning and running wildly back to us.

Big Plume hurried over to where he lay and dismounting beside him, raised him up in his arms. The rest of us made short work of the war party. One or two of them succeeded in reloading their guns and firing at us, but they did no damage and fell one after another, riddled with bullets from our Henry and Winchester repeaters. They were Assiniboins, of course, sneaking around in the cold and snow of winter as usual. My Piegan companions were for once quiet over their success; they felt badly over the fall of Moccasin and quickly scalping and taking the weapons of the dead, they gathered around him in mute sympathy. It was plain that he had made his last run. Cold as it was, beads of perspiration gathered on his pale face, and he writhed in pain. He had been shot in the abdomen. His horse had been caught and stood with the others nearby. "Help me to get into the saddle," he said faintly. "I must get home. I want to see my woman and my little girl before I die. I must see them. Help me up."

Old Big Plume was crying. He had raised the young man

and been father to him. "I can do nothing," he sobbed, "nothing. Some of you lift him up. Someone ride ahead and tell them what has happened."

"No," the wounded man said, "no one shall go first; they will learn about it soon enough. I am badly hurt, I know, but I am going to live to reach my lodge."

We got him up into the saddle and one, mounting behind, supported his drooping form. Another led the horse, and thus we started home. Twice he fainted, and we stopped in a sheltered coulée, spread blankets and laid him on them, bathed his brow with snow and fed him snow when he revived. He was thirsty, calling for water continually. The way seemed terribly long and coming night added to the general gloom of our party. We had started out so happily, had been so successful, and then in an instant death had come among us, our swift home-going had been changed into a funeral trail.

We came to the edge of camp at dusk and filed in past the lodges. People gathered and inquired what had happened. We told them, and some ran on ahead spreading the news. Before we came, Moccasin's wife ran from her lodge to meet us, sobbing heartbrokenly, cautioning us to be careful and carry him in as easily as possible. We laid him on his couch, and she leaned over and held him to her bosom, kissed him fervently, and called on the Sun to let him live. I went out and to my own lodge. Nät-ah'-ki met me at the doorway. She, too, was crying, for Moccasin was a distant relative. She looked anxiously at the blood on my clothes.

"Oh," she gasped, "and they have shot you, too? Show me, quick, where is it? Let me call for help."

"It is nothing," I told her, "nothing but blood from my kill. I am as well as ever."

"But you might have been killed," she cried. "You might have been killed. You are not going hunting any more in this country of war parties. You have no business to hunt. You are a trader, and you are going to stay right here with me where it is safe to live."

Moccasin, poor fellow, died in less than an hour after we got

him home. It was a sad time for us all. Three of the kindliest
and best loved ones in the whole tribe had gone in so short a
time, in such an unlooked-for manner.

We did not get all of the robes that were tanned that winter;
whisky traders occasionally visited the camp and by giving
large quantities of very bad liquor, bartered for some of them.
The Piegans also made frequent trips to Fort Benton to trade.
But we did get 2,200 robes, to say nothing of deer, elk, beaver,
and other pelts, and were well satisfied. The first of April we
were home again at Fort Conrad, and Berry began at once to
tear up the big bottom with his bull teams. Nights he used up
many sheets of paper figuring the profit in raising oats, sixty
bushels to the acre, and in pork-raising—sixteen pigs to the
sow twice a year—anyhow, it all seemed very plain, and sure,
on paper. More plows were bought, some Berkshire pigs were
ordered from the States, a ditch was dug to tap the Dry Fork
of the Marias. We were going to be farmers for sure.

Away down at the end of the bottom, where the Dry Fork
and the Marias met, the women planted their little garden and
erected a brush-roofed summer house, under which they would
sit in the heat of the day and watch their corn and pumpkins
grow, morning and evening faithfully irrigating them with
buckets of water. Time and again Nät-ah'-ki would say: "What
happiness; what peace. Let us pray that it may last."

The Piegans drifted westward from the Bear's Paw country
and most of them returned to their agency, which was now
located on Badger Creek, a tributary of the Marias, about fifty
miles above the Fort. Reports from the agency told of hard
times up there. The agent was said to be starving the people,
and they were already talking of moving back to the buffalo
country.

CHAPTER 24

Nät-ah'-ki's Ride

WEEK after week, the Piegans waited for the buffalo to reappear on the plains of their reservation. With the hot weather they thought that some of the herds to the eastward would stray up to the cooler altitude, and they still believed that somewhere in the unknown fastnesses of the Rockies hordes of the animals had been cached, and that in some way they would be able to return to the open country. In the meantime the hunters scoured the foothills in quest of deer and elk and antelope, finding some, it is true, but barely enough to keep their families from actual starvation.

In our ranching work we were no more successful than the hunters in the chase. There were no rains, with the result that the Dry Fork remained dry, and our irrigating ditch was useless. The thoroughbred Berkshires we procured from the States brought with them, or contracted en route, some disease, and all died except the boar. He finally succumbed, after feasting upon the month's-old carcass of a strychnined wolf. All this was annoying to Berry, but I must confess that I did not feel very badly about it. I was never cut out for a tiller of the soil, and I hoped that this experience would prove to him that he

was not, either. Our few cattle roamed the bottoms and the
nearby hills, waxed fat on the short grama grass and increased.
Who would plough, and sow, and reap in preference to sitting
in the shade and watching a bunch of cattle grow?

Long bull trains trekked down into the bottom, and I sold
the dust-powdered bull-whackers beer, and buckskins, and tobacco. I bought deer and antelope skins from the Indians.

In June the river was bank-full from the melting snow of
the Rockies, and our cable ferry was used by all travelers. One
day I had to cross a bull train, and for the first trip seven yokes
of bulls were driven on board, all the yokes attached to the
long lead chain with which they pulled the wagons. I took the
wheel, the ropes were cast off, and we left the shore, the bull-
whacker of the team standing beside me. He was a French
creole, a voluble, excitable, nervous man, as are most of his
kind. When midway in the stream, where the water was deepest
and swiftest, the lead yoke of bulls backed into the next one,
they into the one behind them, and so on until they were all
huddled to the rear of the boat, and their great weight threw
the bow and upper side of the craft clear above the surface of
the stream. Water poured into the hold through the submerged
deck, and the increasing weight of it tilted the bow higher and
higher until the bulls could no longer retain their footing and
they began to slide off.

"Oh, *mon Dieu!*" the bull-whacker cried, "it is that they will
drown, that they will in the chain entangle. Return, *m'sieur,*
return to the shore!"

But I could do nothing, the boat would go neither forward
nor back, and kept settling deeper in the water, which gurgled
ominously under us. The bulls finally slid off en masse, and
how they did roll and snort and paw, often entirely submerged,
but, strange to say, they drifted down to a bar and waded safely
out in spite of the dangerous chain to which their yokes were
attached. Freed from their weight, the ferry surged the other
way, dived into the stream as it were, and the strong current
bore it down.

"Oh, *mon Dieu!*" the Frenchman cried. "Save me, *m'sieur*. I cannot swim."

And he ran toward me with outstretched arms. I sprang backward to avoid his threatened embrace and fell, and the water sweeping over the deck carried me with it. I didn't mind that much, for I knew that the current would take me to the bar where the bulls had landed. I looked back at the Frenchman. The boat was now deep under the water and he had perched on the center hog-chain post, which was itself only a couple of feet above the surface. I can see him to this day, sitting there on top of the post, his eyes saucerlike with terror, the ends of his fierce mustache pointing to heaven, and I can still hear him, as he repeatedly crossed himself, alternately praying and cursing and calling on his comrades ashore to save him from the turbid flood. He was such a funny sight that I laughed so I could hardly keep my head above the water.

"Hang on, Frenchy!" cried the wagon boss and others. "Just hang on, you'll come out all right."

He shook his fist at them. "H' I am sink. H' I am drown. You maudit whack eet de bull," he answered "an' you tell me hang on. Oh, *sacré!* Oh, *misère!* Oh, *mon Dieu!*"

I doubt not that he might have let go and sunk had the boat settled any deeper in the water, but just then the cable parted and it rose so that the deck was barely awash, and drifted along after me. Down jumped Frenchy and pirouetted around on its slippery surface, and shouted and laughed for joy, snapped his fingers at the men who had jeered him, and cried: "*Adieu, adieu, messieurs;* me, I am bound for St. Louis, an' my sweetheart."

The boat drifted ashore not far below, and we had no difficulty in towing it back and repairing the cable. Frenchy, however, would not cross with his bulls, but went over with a load of the wagons, and he took a plank with him, to use as a float in case of accident....

In the hot summer nights Nät-ah'-ki and I slept out on the edge of a high-cut bank near the river. Oh, those white, moonlit perfect nights! They were so perfect, so peaceful, that the beauty and wonder of it all kept us awake long after we should have been sleeping soundly. An owl hooted. "'Tis the ghost of some unfortunate one," she would say. "For some wrong he did, his shadow became an owl, and he must long suffer, afraid of the Sun, mournfully crying of nights, before he can at last join the other shadows of our people who have gone on to the Sand-hills."

A wolf howled. "Oh, brother, why so sad? It seems as if they are always crying for something that has been taken from them, or that they have lost. Will they ever find it, I wonder?"

The river now moved and gurgled under the bank, and roared hollow down the rapid in the bend below. A beaver, or perchance a big fish, splashed its silvery surface, and she would nestle closer, shivering. "'Tis the people of the deep waters," she would whisper. "Why, I wonder, was it given them to live away down in the deep, dark, cold places, instead of on the land and in the bright sunlight? Do you think they are happy and warm and content, as we are?"

Such questions I answered to the best of my ability. "The goat loves the high, cold, bare cliffs of the mountains," I said to her, "the antelope the warm, low, bare plains. No doubt the people of the river love its depths, or they would live on the land as we do."

One night, after listening to the hooting of a big owl up on the island, she said; "Just think how unhappy that shadow is, and even were it permitted to go on to the Sandhills, still it would be unhappy. They are all unhappy there, our people who have gone from us, living their shadow, make-believe lives. That is why I do not want to die. It is so cold and cheerless there, and your shadow could not be with me. White men's shadows cannot enter the home of the Blackfeet dead."

I said nothing, and after a little she continued: "Tell me, can it really be true that which the Black Robes say about the next life, that the good people, Indian and white, will go away up in the sky then and live happily with World Maker forever?"

What could I do but encourage her? "What they say," I replied, "is written in their ancient book. They believe it. Yes, they do believe it, and I do, too. I am glad to believe it. We can still be together after this life is over."

As the summer wore on the question of food became very serious to the Piegans, and we heard that the more northern tribes of the Blackfeet were also suffering. The Piegan agent, in his annual report to the Department of the Interior, had deplored the barbarism of his charges, their heathenish worship of strange gods, but he told nothing of their physical needs. "I have nothing for you," he said to the chiefs. "Take your people to buffalo and follow the herds."

This was in August. They all moved down near our place, and while the hunters rode the plains after antelope, the chiefs conferred with Berry, planning for the winter. They finally decided to move to the Judith country, where the buffalo were thought to be still plentiful and where there were practically as many elk and deer, beaver and wolves as ever. In September we also trailed out, Berry, the Crow Woman, Nät-ah'-ki and I, and in a week or more went into camp on the Judith River, only a mile or two above the mouth of Warm Spring Creek.

In Fort Benton we had engaged a couple of extra men, and with their help we soon threw up a row of log cabins and a couple of rude fireplaces. We were located in the heart of an extensive cottonwood grove, sheltered from the northern winds, and right beside us ran the river, then fairly alive with big, fat trout. According to agreement, the Piegans came and pitched their lodges near us, and a part of the Blood tribe moved down from the north and mixed with them.

Nät-ah'-ki and I went once after buffalo, camping with Red Bird's Tail, a genial man of thirty-five or forty. There were few lodges, but many people, and we traveled as light as possible. We found buffalo toward the close of the first day out, but went on until noon of the next, and camped on the head of Armells Creek. From a little butte nearby we could see that the prairie was black with them clear to the breaks of the Missouri, and to the eastward where the buttes of Big Crooked Creek and the Musselshell loomed in the distance. The Moccasin Mountains shut off the view of the south, but westward there were also buffalo.

"Ha!" exclaimed Red Bird's Tail, who had ridden up beside me. "Who says the buffalo are about gone? Why, it is as it has always been; the land is dark with them. Never have I seen them more plentiful."

"Remember that we have come far to find them," I told him; "that the plains to the west, and away in the north, are barren of them."

"Ah, that is true, but it will not be for long; they must have all moved eastward for a time as our fathers tell us once happened before. They will go back again. Surely, the good Sun will not forget us."

I had not the heart to destroy his hopes, to tell him of the vast regions to the east and south of us, where there were no longer any buffalo, where the antelope, even, had been practically exterminated.

Red Bird's Tail was the leader of our party, and the hunters were subject to his orders. We had ridden out on to the butte very early, and after getting a view of the country and the position of the herds, he decided that a certain herd southwest of us should be chased, as they would run westward into the wind, and not disturb the larger ones. The lay of the land was favorable and we succeeded in riding right into the edge of the herd before they became alarmed, and then they ran, as Red Bird's Tail had predicted, into the wind and up a long slope, an outlying ridge of the mountains. That gave us an advantage, as the buffalo were not swift runners on an up-grade. On a downhill run, however, they could easily outstrip the swiftest horse. All their weight was forward; there was not enough strength in their small, low hindquarters to propel their abnormally deep chests, huge heads, and heavy hump with any noticeable speed when they went uphill.

Nät-ah'-ki was riding a gentle little mare which had been loaned her by one of our Blood friends for the trip. All the way from the Judith she kept plying her quirt and calling it sundry reproachful names, in order to keep it beside my more spirited mount. But the moment we came near the herd, and the hunters dashed into it, the animal suddenly reared up, pranced sideways with arching neck and twitching ears, and then, getting the bit firmly in its teeth, it sprang out into the chase as madly as any other of the trained runners. Indeed, that is what it was, a well-trained buffalo horse, but the owner had not thought to tell us so. It was even swifter than mine, and I felt no little anxiety as I saw it carry her into that sea of madly running, shaggy-backed animals. In vain I urged my horse; I could not overtake her, and my warning shouts were lost in the thunder and rattle of a thousand hoofs. I soon saw that she was not trying to hold in the animal, but was quirting it instead, and once she looked back at me and laughed, her eyes shining with excitement. On we went, up the slope for a mile or more, and then the scattering herd drew away from us and went flying down the other side of the ridge.

"What made you do it?" I asked as we checked up our sweating, panting horses. "Why did you do it? I was so afraid you would get a fall, perhaps be hooked by some of the wounded."

"Well," she replied, "at first I was scared, too, but it was such fun, riding after them. Just think of it, I struck four of them with my quirt! I just wanted to keep on, and I never thought of badger holes, or falling, or anything else. And once a great big cow looked up at me and snorted so hard that I felt her warm breath. Tell me, how many did you kill!"

"Not one," I replied. I hadn't fired a shot; I had noticed nothing, seen nothing but her as she rode in the thick of it all, and I was more than glad when the run ended. We looked back down the slope and saw the hunters and their women already at work on the carcasses of their kill, which dotted the snow. But we—we were meatless. It would never do for us to return to camp without some, so we rode on for a mile or two in the direction the herd had gone, and then turned off into the mountains. Up among the pines there were deer, both kinds, and here and there were groups of elk feeding or lying down in the open parks. While Nät-ah'-ki held my horse I approached some of the elk, and by good luck killed a fat, dry cow. We built a fire and roasted some of the liver and a piece of tripe, and, after a hasty meal, rode back to camp with all the meat our horses could conveniently pack.

CHAPTER 25

Curbing the Wanderers

WE made another run the next day. The sun shone bright and warm, there was a big herd of buffalo nearby, everyone rode out from camp in the best of spirits. I had changed horses with Nät-ah'-ki; while mine liked to run as well as hers, it had a tender mouth, and she could easily control it. Once into the herd, I paid no attention to anyone else, but did my best to single out the fat cows, overtake and kill them. I did not need the meat nor robes, but there were those with us who had poor mounts, and what I killed I intended to give them. So I urged the little mare on, and managed to kill seven head.

When I stopped at last, no one was near me; looking back I saw the people gathered in two groups, and from the largest and nearest one arose the distressing wailing of the women for the dead. I soon learned the cause of it all; Young Arrow Maker had been killed, his horse disembowelled; Two Bows had been thrown and his leg was broken. A huge old bull, wounded and mad with pain, had lunged into Arrow Maker's horse, tearing out its flank and knocking the rider off on to the backs of its close-pursuing mates, and he had been trampled to death by the frantic-running herd.

Two Bows' horse had stepped into a badger hole and he had
been hurled to the ground, his right leg broken above the knee.
Some of the women's horses were dragging travois, and we laid
the dead and the injured on them and they were taken to camp
by their relatives. We hurried to skin the dead buffalo, some
of the hunters taking no more of the meat than the tongue and
boss ribs, and then we also went back to the lodges, silently
and quietly. There was no feasting and singing that night.

They buried Arrow Maker in the morning, placing the body
in the fork of a big cottonwood, and then we prepared to move
camp, which took all the rest of the day, as meat was cut and
dried to reduce weight, and the many hides had to be trimmed,
the frozen ones thawed and folded for packing. There was not
a man in camp who knew anything about mending a broken
leg, but we splinted and bound Two Bows' fracture as best we
could. On the succeeding morning we broke camp early and
started homeward, every one frantic to get away from the unlucky place before more misfortune should happen. The injured
man was made as comfortable as possible on a couch lashed to
a travois.

In the afternoon a blizzard set in, a bitterly cold one, which
drifted and whirled the fine snow in clouds around us. A few
decided to make camp in the first patch of timber we should
come to, but the rest declared that they would keep on through
the night until they arrived home. They were afraid to stop;
more afraid of some dread misfortune overtaking them than
they were of Cold Maker's blinding snow and intense cold. Evil
spirits, they reasoned, hovered near them, had already caused
death and suffering, and none would be safe until the hunt was
ended and sacrifices made to the gods. Red Bird's Tail was one
of those who elected to keep on.

The low flying snow-spitting clouds hid the moon as we hung
on to our saddles and gave our horses the reins, trusting them
to keep in the trail which Red Bird's Tail broke for us. We could
not have guided them had we wished to, for our hands became
so numb we were obliged to fold them in the robes and blankets
which enveloped us. I rode directly behind Nät-ah'-ki, she next

after our leader, whose family followed us. Looking back, I could see them sometimes, but more often they were hidden in the blinding snow.

Red Bird's Tail and many of the other men frequently sprang from their horses and walked, even ran, in vain effort to keep warm, but the women remained in the saddle and shivered, and some froze hands and faces. While still some six or eight miles from home, Red Bird's Tail, walking ahead of his horse, dropped into a spring, over which the snow had drifted. The water was waist-deep and froze on his leggings the instant he climbed out of the hole; but he made no complaint, walking sturdily on through the deepening drifts until we finally arrived home. It was all I could do to dismount, I was so stiff and cramped and cold; and I had to lift Nät-ah'-ki from her saddle and carry her inside. We had been on the trail something like seventeen hours! I roused one of the men to care for our horses, and we crawled into bed, under half a dozen robes and blankets, shivering so hard that our teeth chattered.

When we awoke it was nearly noon; and we learned that a woman of our party had dropped from her horse and Cold Maker had claimed her for his own. Her body was never found.

I related the experiences of the trip to Berry. "Well," he said, "I warned you not to go. A man who can stay close to the fire in the winter, but leaves it for a hunt out on the plains, is sure locoed. Yes, sir, he's a plumb fool."

In September a man named Charles Walmsley, en route from Fort Macleod to Fort Benton, was found murdered on Cut Bank Creek. His wagon, harness, and other effects had been partly burned and thrown into the stream. Suspicion finally fell upon one Turtle and his companion, The Rider, Blood Indians, who had spent several hundred dollars Canadian money in Fort Benton for guns and various things dear to the Indian's heart. Learning their whereabouts, the sheriff came out to arrest them, bringing with him only the under-sheriff, Jeff Talbot. There may have been braver men on the frontier than Sheriff John J. Healy, but I never met them. He held the office for many terms, and owned the Fort Benton *Record,* the first newspaper printed on the plains of Montana. Previous to this he had been an Indian trader, and was one of the leading men of Whoop-Up and the northern trade; one of the "thieves, murderers, criminals of every stripe," as Miss Laut calls us.

He and Talbot drove in at our place about sundown one evening, and as soon as they had cared for their horses, he told why they had come.

Berry shook his head. "I wouldn't attempt to arrest them here if I were you," he said. "These Bloods are pretty mean, and Turtle has a whole lot of relatives and friends among them. I believe they'll fight. Old man, you'd better go back and get some of the soldiers at the fort to help you."

"I don't give a continental damn if he has a thousand friends and relatives!" Healy exclaimed. "I've come out here after those Indians, and they're going back with me, dead or alive."

"Well," said Berry, "if you are bound to try it, of course we'll stay with you; but I don't like it."

"No, sir," said Healy. "This is my funeral. On account of your trade you can't afford to mix up in it. They'd have it in for you and move away. Come on, Jeff."

They left, and we passed fifteen minutes of pretty acute suspense. We armed our men and ourselves, and stood waiting to go to their aid, although we knew that if anything happened, we would be too late. But while we were talking and keeping a good watch on the camp, Healy and Talbot returned with their men, both securely handcuffed. One they chained to the center post of our trade room, the other to a long wall of the kitchen. "There!" Healy exclaimed. "Haven't you anything to give a hungry man? I'm just starving."

Healy spoke good Blackfoot. When he and Talbot went into the camp he inquired for Running Rabbit, the Blood chief, and they were shown into his lodge, where he quickly stated his business. The old chief said that he would send for the men, and they could have a talk. "But," he concluded, "I can't be answerable for what may happen if you try to take them away. My young men are wild. I can't control them."

The women sent to ask Turtle and The Rider to the chief's lodge had been cautioned to say nothing, to give no reason why they were wanted, and they came in and sat down quite unsuspicious, followed by a number of other men, curious to learn the cause of the white men's visit. Healy soon explained it.

"I don't know anything about it," said Turtle, "and I'm not going with you. I will not go; I'll fight; I've got friends here who will help me."

He had no sooner spoken than Healy, who was a very powerful man, seized him and snapped a pair of handcuffs on his wrists, Talbot doing the same with The Rider. Both of the Indians were furious, and those sitting with them became excited, shouting, "You shall not take them." "We will not let them go." "Take off those iron things, or we will do you harm."

"Listen!" said Healy, holding up his hand warningly. "You all know me; you know I am not afraid. I have got to take these two men with me. I am going to take them. If any of you interfere, I will not be the only one to die. You know how I can shoot, and some of you will die before I do."

He had not pulled his gun; he stared them coldly in the eyes, and when he was aroused those eyes could make even an innocent man shiver.

"Come!" he said to Turtle, and the Indian mechanically arose and followed him out, Talbot and the other following.

None of us slept much that night. Late in the evening a Piegan youth came in and told us that the Bloods were planning to rescue their friends, some proposing to attack the trading post, others saying that it would be better to waylay the officers on the trail next day. "You go back and tell them that I hope they'll try it," said Healy. "We've got some Winchesters and six-shooters, and plenty of cartridges, and we'll have a real good time. Turtle and The Rider here will get our first two bullets."

The prisoners were taken safely to Helena, and at the trial, The Rider turned state's evidence; Turtle had shot Walmsley in the back while he was cooking supper. He got imprisonment for life, and died two years later in the penitentiary in Detroit.

No white man has since been killed by any Indians of the Blackfoot tribes.

The winter had been pretty hard, and the Indians did not kill so many buffalo as they would had the herds been nearer camp. Still, they were tanning a good number of robes, and had a large number of rawhides on hand, when, one evening, a detachment of soldiers under command of Lieutenant Crouse arrived from Fort Benton. It was pitiful to see the women and children run to hide in the brush, their eyes wide with fear. The men said nothing, but they seized their weapons and stood about outside of their lodges, ready to fight if need be, until they saw the detachment halt and prepare to camp. It was not to be war then, they concluded, and called in their wives and little ones. But the soldiers' errand was only a degree less serious than would have been a battle. They had come to escort the Piegan's back to their reservation, where there were no buffalo, nor game of any kind, and to fight them if they refused to go. A council was held. "Why, why," asked White Calf, his face ashen with suppressed anger, "is this to be done? By what right? We are on our own ground. It was always ours. Who shall say that we must leave it?"

Lieutenant Crouse told them that he was but an unwilling instrument, carrying out the order of his superiors, who in turn had been told by the Great Father himself that they must move the Piegans back to their Agency. Complaint had been made of them. The cattlemen claimed that they were killing their cattle and had requested that they be sent home. The Great Father had listened to their demand.

"Listen!" said White Calf. "Years ago there came some of the Great Father's men on a steamboat to the mouth of the Judith River, and there they made a treaty with our people. It was made on paper, which they and our chiefs put their names on. I was a young man then, but I had understanding and I well remember what was put on that paper in the white man's writing. It said that all the land lying north of the Musselshell River and the Missouri as far as the mouth of Milk

River, up to the Canadian line, from the Rockies eastward to
a line running north from the mouth of Mill River—all that
country, it said, was ours. Since that time the whites have
never bought any of it, nor even asked us for any. How then,
can they say that we shall not hunt here?

"We are accused of killing cattle! We have not done so. Why
should we when we have fat buffalo and deer and elk and other
game, fat animals, all whose hides are useful! We do not wish
to return to our agency. The man there has nothing for us.
There is no game in that region. If we go, we must starve. It
is a dreadful thing to suffer for want of food. Pity our little
children, our women, and our aged ones. Go back to your fort
and leave us in peace."

Others arose and talked, and their pleas to be allowed to
remain in the game country were pathetic. I am sure that there
was a catch in the lieutenant's voice when he replied that he
was powerless to do as they wished, and he asked them not to
make it any harder for him by refusing to go. He then arose
and left the council, asking to be informed soon what they
concluded to do.

It did not take long to decide. "Of course," said White Calf,
"we could kill the soldiers here, but others, many more, would
replace them. They would kill off our women and children, even
the new-born babies, as they did before on the Marias. No, we
cannot fight them. Let us go back to the agency and try in some
way to procure food."

A couple of days later the lodges came down, we packed our
robes and various impedimenta into wagons and abandoned
the camp, and all took the trail for the north, escorted by the
soldiers. This was in March, and the Indians' stock was so worn
and poor that they could travel only twelve or fifteen miles a
day, and hundreds of horses died along the trail. Heavily loaded
as were our wagons, we made even better time than they, and
arrived in Fort Benton ahead of them. Our total trade amounted
to eight hundred robes, three thousand deer, elk, and antelope
hides, and I forget how many beaver and wolf skins.

From Fort Benton the Indians journeyed slowly out to our

place, Fort Conrad, and thence straggled on up to their agency, where the women tanned their rawhides, and from the sale of the robes they kept from actual starvation for a time.

The true explanation of this unjust treatment of the Piegans is simply that the owners of the cattle ranch on Big Spring Creek also owned the traders' post at the agency; they wanted to have the Indians back there, knowing that they would get hundreds of robes from them. So they trumped up the charge that the Piegans were slaughtering their cattle, and having powerful influence in Washington, their complaint was acted upon. They got the robes all right, and then, seeing the successful trade they were doing, they induced an innocent pilgrim to purchase the tradership from them. He got an empty bag, for by midsummer the Piegans hadn't a single robe to sell, nor anything else with which to purchase a pound of tea.

CHAPTER 26

Crees and Red Rivers

HOME again at Fort Conrad. Somehow Nät-ah′-ki and I liked that place better than any we had lived in. The river, murmuring and gurgling by our window, the lovely green groves in the grassy bottoms, the sloping rise of the valley, the rude room itself built of massive logs, cool in summer, warm in winter and alight with the blaze in the hearth, seemed to us all that we could desire. "Let us never leave here again," she said; "let us stay right here in peace and comfort."

But I told her, as I had before, that we could not always do as we wished; that in a few weeks, or months, we might be obliged to take the trail to buffalo again.

Berry made a flying trip through the buffalo country in May, and upon his return we made preparations to establish a trading post on the Missouri at Carrol, a hundred and fifty miles below Fort Benton. Steele and Broadwater, partners in the Diamond R outfit, a great transportation company, had started the place some years before with the view of hauling freight from the steamboats there directly to Helena, but this plan had failed, and their buildings had long since fallen into the ever-

encroaching river. We chose the location because it lay south
of the Little Rocky Mountains, north of the Snowies, had good
wagon roads leading out of it, and above all because it seemed
to be in the very center of the remaining buffalo country. We
sent a trusted Indian north into Canada to notify the Blackfeet
and Bloods of our intention, and they agreed to move down
there as soon as possible. So did our near neighbors, the Piegans. We counted on having a big trade.

It was the first part of July, 1880, that we arrived at Carrol
by boat from Fort Benton. We had tons of trade goods aboard.
Berry's bull train had preceded us overland, and the men had
already put up a commodious two-room cabin, which was to be
our kitchen and dining room. We took possession of it at once,
and the women cooked us a good meal.

By the middle of September we were in good shape for the
winter, having built a large log store and warehouse, a smoke-
house for curing buffalo tongues, and a row of sleeping quarters.
True to their promise, the Blackfeet and Bloods came down
from the north, and a little later there came about two thousand
Canadian Crees, under Chief Big Bear. There also trailed in
a large number of Red River French and English halfbreeds
with their awkward, creaking, two-wheel carts.

An opposition trader had started a small store about two
hundred yards above us. He had never been in the Indian trade,
but boasted of his commercial successes in the States, and said
that he would soon put us out of business, even if he did not
have such a large stock of goods. When the Blackfeet appeared
on the opposite side of the river, he went across and invited
the chiefs to feast with him. They all got into his boat and came
over, but the moment they stepped ashore a beeline was made
for our place, and the welcome they well knew awaited them.

The North Blackfeet were friendly with the Crees; had in-
termarried with them to some extent. The two tribes camped
side by side in the bottoms near us all winter. The Bloods,
however, were not so friendly to them, and hunted out south
of the river, along the foot of the Snowies. The chiefs of the two
tribes made a sort of armistice, agreeing that for the winter,

at least, there should be no trouble between them. But the Piegans would not meet their long-time enemy, and hunted in the country to the west of us, occasionally sending out a war party to kill a few of the Crees and drive off their stock. We got none of their trade.

Nät-ah'-ki and the Crow Woman were highly indignant when they saw the Crees pull in from the north. "By what right," asked the latter, "are they here. The soldiers ought to drive them back to their brush swamps. It is wrong to allow them to kill the buffalo and other game belonging to our people."

Even more than the Crees, I disliked their half brothers, the French-Cree Red River breeds. They were not dark, but actually black-skinned, and they dressed in black, both women and men, the latter wearing a bright red sash around the waist. The women's kerchiefs were black. And then the men had such a despicable way of wearing their hair, cut straight off just above the shoulders, and standing out around the head like a huge mop.

But it was not for their looks that I disliked them so much as it was their habits and customs. They ate dogs, for one thing; they pretended to be faithful and zealous members of the church, but were the worst set of liars and thieves that ever traveled across the plains; they hated the Americans as much as they did the English, and in their bastard French cursed us until, one day, I could stand it no longer. I jumped over the counter and struck one of them, a fellow named Amiott, a stinging blow in the cheek which sent him sprawling to the floor.

"That is for your cursing of us," I told him. "I will not hear any more of it in this place. If you don't like it, you and the others here go and heel yourselves and come back."

Strange to say, we did not lose any trade by this. The very ones I had called down remained our customers, and quiet ones they were, too.

Louis Riel! How well and yet how little I knew him, he who led the half-breed rebellion of 1885 in Canada. He was a fine-looking man, even if his bright black eyes were a bit shifty, and he had such courtly manners. When still thirty or forty yards away he would remove his wide sombrero with a grand sweep and approach you bowing and smiling, and filling the air with high-flown compliments. He had a fine education; the Jesuits having trained him for the priesthood, but certain lapses had prevented his ordination.

It was his education, I believe, which caused his downfall, for he overestimated himself and his power. Still, I was never able to determine whether he really believed in his cause and his power to right what he called the wrongs of his oppressed and defrauded people, or whether he got up the row, expecting to be bought off by the Canadian government and to live in wealth ever afterward. He came to us with his people from the plains of the north and soon got into Berry's good graces, for he was an exceedingly smooth and persuasive talker. He wanted some goods on credit with which to trade in his camp, and got them. We kept an open account with him for nearly two years. It is still open, for he vanished between sun and sun, owing a balance of seven hundred dollars.

"Well," said Berry, "we are about even. He must have bowed to us about seven hundred times, and I reckon that such grand and low bows as those are worth about a dollar apiece."

None of the Red River half-breeds, save Riel, had the slightest conception of the power of the Canadian, and back of that, the English people. But he knew, for he had been eastward to Ottawa, Montreal, and Quebec, and from his reading had acquired an all-round knowledge of the world in general. Yet there at our place he held meeting after meeting and wrought his people up to the highest pitch, telling them that the Canadian-English were few and inexperienced, and that in a few weeks they could subdue them by force of arms. Asked for our opinion, we told them that they had no earthly chance to win, and so did a Catholic priest, Father Scullin, who lived with us.

Had the buffalo lasted, I doubt if Riel would have succeeded in getting the Red Rivers to revolt. But when they began to starve, they became desperate and broke out. The whole body of them, Crees and Red Rivers, did not put up as good a fight as a handful of Blackfeet would have made, and Riel was tried, condemned, and hanged for treason.

Some of the French breed women were exceedingly lovely, even in the sombre and outlandish garb they wore. There was Amelie, for instance, whose husband, a Frenchman, was killed in a buffalo chase. Every young French breed in camp was courting her, but she told them to leave her alone. "I don't want no more French mans," she told us. "I don't want no H'Injun, no H'Englis mans. I want Americane mans, me."

Long John Pape and Mike Duval fought over her, and the former was badly whipped. Mike thought then that he had her sure, and was begging her to name the day, when one morning Billy Burns walked into her cabin, picked her up in his arms without a word, and carrying her over to our place, he set her on her feet before the astonished priest. "Just hitch us up," he said, "and be quick about it."

"I won't!" Amelie screamed, giving him a resounding slap in the face. "I won't! Go way from me, you bad mans! Let me alone!"

"Oh, well," said Billy, "if you won't, of course you won't. I thought you kind o' liked me."

He turned abruptly and started for the door, but Amelie ran after him and grasped his arm. "Come back, you big fools!" she commanded, with a stamp of her pretty, moccasined foot. "Come back! Me, h'I'm only make it joke; course I marry you; you got blue h'eyes."

They stood again before the priest and he married them then and there.

Such a blowout as there was that night. Long John and Duval not only made friends, but when Nät-ah'-ki and I looked in for a moment, they were weeping on each other's shoulders. Billy and Amelie had fled. Having provided the cabin, the musicians, the solid and liquid refreshments for the party, they hitched a horse to a half-breed sled and sped away down the river to the camp of a friend. . . .

I think the Crees and Red Rivers loved liquor more than any

other people I met on the plains. The Blackfeet liked it, but
not well enough to impoverish themselves for it. The former,
however, would sell anything they had to obtain it, even their
women, and it was rare for a family to have more than half a
dozen horses. Many of the Crees were obliged to walk when
moving camp, packing their few effects on dogs. They were not
lazy, however, and killed and tanned a great many robes which
they exchanged for liquor, tea, and tobacco, seldom buying any
finery. There were nights when at least a thousand of them
would be drunk together, dancing and singing around little
fires built down in the timber, some crying foolishly, some
making love, others going through all sorts of strange and
uncouth antics. There was very little quarreling among them,
not half a dozen being killed in the whole winter. More than
that number froze to death, falling on their way in the night
and being unable to rise and go on.

CHAPTER 27

The Last of the Buffalo

WHEN spring came, the Blackfeet and Bloods moved back into Canada in order to get their treaty money from the Government. The Crees and Red Rivers remained with us. Our trade for the season yielded four thousand buffalo robes and about an equal number of deer, elk, and antelope skins. For the robes we received $28,000, for the skins, some beaver and wolf pelts about $5,000 more. That was our banner season, and the biggest one Berry had ever experienced.

We were looking forward to a quiet summer, as usual, when orders came from the Sioux Agency Indian traders of Dakota, and from firms in the Northwest Territory of Canada for pemmican and dried meat. The letters all had the same story to tell. "The buffalo are gone," they said. "Send us as many tons of the stuff as you can for our trade." The Crees and their half-brothers were happy when we told them that we would buy all they could bring us, and they lost no time in beginning to hunt. Everything went that was meat—poor cows, old bulls, and perhaps crippled horses. The meat was dried in wide, thin, flat sheets, and done up in rawhide-thonged bales. Pemmican was made by pounding the dried meat into fragments and mixing it with tallow and grease extracted from the animals' bones. It was packed into flat, oblong bags of green hide and the covering shrunk so tightly over the mass as it dried that a package of it had the solidity and weight of a rock. I do not remember how much of the stuff we got during the summer, literally cords and cords of the dried meat and hundreds of bags of pemmican, all of which we sold at a good profit.

One day in midsummer a tall, slender man came to our place. His face and the black, sharp-ended, up-curling mustache he wore reminded one of pictures of the old-time Spanish cavaliers. He spoke English, pure English, much better, indeed, than that of any white man around, better than many West Point graduates of the army. He introduced himself as William Jackson. The name seemed familiar, but I could not place him until he said that he was sometimes called Sik-si-ka'-kwan— Blackfoot Man. Then I knew. How often I had heard old man Monroe mention his favorite grandson, his bravery and kindness of heart. We became lasting friends, friends to the day of his death, and I hope that together we accomplished some measure of good in penance for our many sins.

No one can make me believe that there is nothing in heredity. There was Jackson, for instance. On his mother's side, he came from the Monroes, a notedly brave family of Scotch Highlanders, and from the La Roches, a noble French family, some of whom early emigrated to America. His father, Thomas Jackson, had taken part in the Seminole and other Indian wars of 1832. His great grandfathers on both sides had fought in the Revolution. No wonder, then, that he took to war as a profession, enlisting at an early age as scout in the United States Army.

The summer previous to his enlistment he made a name for himself by killing three Sioux. He and his mother went berrying in the breaks of the river north of Fort Union. Four or five miles away they saw five Sioux sneaking down on them, following a deep coulée running parallel with the ridge upon which they were riding.

Jackson kept on a little way, gradually riding off to the west side of the ridge and out of sight of the enemy. Then he told his mother what he had seen, made her take his horse, the stronger and swifter of the two, and told her to ride back to the Fort for help as swiftly as she could. Jackson at once went up to the top of the ridge, peering over it very carefully. In a moment the Sioux mounted and burst out of the brush full tilt after his mother.

There was his chance, and kneeling to get a steady aim, he fired his Henry rifle a number of times, dropping two of the enemy. But that did not stop the others, who came swiftly up the ridge, so Jackson mounted his horse and took the back trail. The rider of the best horse kept gaining on him, firing his muzzle-loader as fast as he could, and Jackson kept shooting back at short intervals, failing also to hit his foe. Finally, when the Sioux had lessened the gap between them to about a hundred yards, Jackson stopped his horse, and jumping off, knelt down and took a careful aim at his pursuer. The Sioux never stopped but whipped his horse harder than ever, Jackson fired twice at him. The second shot hit him fairly in the breast and he tumbled to the ground, where he lay perfectly still. Then Jackson remounted and rode on. The remaining two Sioux pursued him for half a mile or so, when they stopped, talked together for a moment, and turned back to take care of their dead.

Jackson was a favorite with the army officers, especially Generals Custer and Miles. On the morning of the battle of the Little Big Horn, June 25, 1876, he, with the other scouts, was detailed to accompany Major Reno. Had they accompanied Custer, they would have undoubtedly shared his fate. As it was, they did what they could—at the expense of the lives of most of them—to save Reno and his command from utter annihilation. When the Sioux charged, they held their ground for a time to give the soldiers a chance to retreat across the river and up the hill, where they were nearly overcome several times by the enemy. Jackson was finally cut off from the command with Lieutenant DeRudio, Interpreter Girard, and a soldier. They lay in the thick brush all that day and the next.

When evening came Jackson ventured out, took leggings and blankets from the bodies of the Sioux, and when they had dressed themselves and wrapped blankets about themselves, he led them right through the watchfires of the Sioux to their comrades up on the hill.

Only once were they accosted. "Who goes there?" asked someone sitting by a small fire roasting meat.

Jackson, who spoke Sioux perfectly, replied, "It is only us, we're going over here a little way."

"Well, go where you're going," said their questioner. "I'm going to sit right here and eat some meat."

At the time he came to the store at Carrol, Jackson was trading with the Indians out near the Judith Mountains. I was sorry to part with him. I hardly expected to meet him again, but I did some years afterward on the reservation where all the "squawmen," as we were called, were driven by the tenderfeet, the "pilgrims," with their five-cent ways of doing business.

Winter came again, and the Crees and Red River breeds were still with us, but the buffalo were not so plentiful as they had been the previous winter. Their range was also smaller, extending from the mouth of Judith River eastward to the Round Butte, on the north side of the Missouri, one hundred and twenty-five miles, and back from the river not more than forty miles. They were far more plentiful on the south side, between the Missouri and the Yellowstone, but so were the hunters. The white hunters were the most destructive of all, and piled up more than one hundred thousand buffalo hides along the Yellowstone that winter, which they sold for about two dollars each to Eastern tannery buyers. As the season advanced, the hunters had to ride farther and farther to find the game. There was no doubt but that the end of the trade was near.

In February we ran short of trade blankets, and I went to a trading post up at the mouth of the Judith after more, taking Nät-ah'-ki with me. The river was solidly frozen, so we took that route, each driving a pony hitched to a Red River sled.

We reached our destination, and the following day started home with our loads of blankets. It was about four in the afternoon that we saw some buffalo scurrying southward across the river, and heard some firing back in the breaks. A little later we saw a large camp of Indians file down into a bottom below us. Nät-ah'-ki gazed at them intently for a moment; they were already pitching their lodges, and a painted lodge-skin was just then elevated and spread around the poles. "Oh!" she cried, with a happy catch of the breath which was almost a sob, "Oh, they are our people. See! that is the buffalo medicine lodge they have put up."

They were indeed some of the Piegans under Red Bird's Tail, with whom we camped that night. They were as pleased to meet us as we were them, and it was far into the night when we reluctantly went to bed, the supply of lodge fuel having given out. "We are near the end of it," Red Bird's Tail said to me. "We have hunted far this winter, along Milk River, in the Wolf Mountains (Little Rockies), and now over here on the Big River, and we have just about had meat enough to eat. Friend, I fear that this is our last buffalo hunt."

I told him of the conditions south and east of us, that there were no buffalo anywhere, except the few between us and the Yellowstone, and even there no herds of more than a hundred or so. "Are you sure," he said; "sure that the white men have seen all the land which they say lies between the two salt waters? Haven't they overlooked some big part of the country where our buffalo have congregated and from whence they may return?"

"There is no place in the whole land," I replied, "north, south, east, or west, that the white men have not traveled, are not traveling right now, and none of them can find buffalo. White men are just as anxious to kill buffalo for their hides and meat as you are."

On our way homeward the next morning, I saw a lone buffalo calf—almost a yearling—standing forlornly in a clump of rye grass near the river. I killed it, and took off the hide, horns, hoofs, and all. The Crow Woman tanned it for me later and decorated the flesh side with gaudy porcupine quill work. That was my last buffalo. Along in the afternoon we startled something like seventy-five head which had come to the frozen stream in search of water. They scampered wildly across the bottom and up the slope of the valley to the plains. That was the last herd of them that Nät-ah'-ki and I ever saw.

CHAPTER 28

The Winter of Death

BACK home on the Marias, we had Piegans with us from time to time, and they told harrowing tales of hard times up at their agency. The weekly rations, they said, lasted but one day. There was no game of any kind to be found; their agent would give them nothing. Those with us and scattered along the river, by hard hunting found deer and antelope enough to keep themselves alive, but those remaining at the agency actually suffered for want of food. They were the ones who could not get away. They had lost their horses through a skin disease which had spread among the herds, or had sold them to the trader for provisions.

In September Nät-ah'-ki and I went up to the agency to see for ourselves what was the condition of affairs. Arriving at the main camp, just below the agency stockade, at dusk, we stopped with old Lodge-pole Chief for the night. "Leave our food sacks with the saddles," I said.

The old man and his wives welcomed us cordially. "Hurry," he commanded the women, "cook a meal for our friends. They must be hungry after their long ride." He smiled happily and rubbed his hands together as he talked.

But his wives did not smile. From a parfleche they brought forth three small potatoes and set them to boil, and from another one, two quarter-pound trout, which they also boiled. After a time they set them before us. "It's all we have," said one of the women.

At that old Lodge-pole Chief broke down. "It is the truth," he said haltingly. "We have nothing. There are no more buffalo, the Great Father sends us but a little food—gone in a day. We are very hungry. There are fish, to be sure—forbidden by the gods, unclean. We eat them, but they do not give us any strength, and I doubt not that we will be punished for eating them. It seems as if our gods had forsaken us."

Nät-ah'-ki went out and brought back one of our food sacks and handed to the women three or four tins of beans, corned beef and corn, some sugar, coffee, and flour. To the old man she gave a piece of tobacco. Their faces brightened and they talked and laughed as they cooked and ate a good meal.

The next day we rode to the various camps and found the same conditions in each. Not actual starvation, but something so near it that the most vigorous of the men and women showed the want of food. They appealed to me for help, and I gave freely what I had; but that of course was a mere nothing, as compared to their needs. Nät-ah'-ki's mother had been long in one of the camps, caring for a sick relative, now dead. We rescued her from the place of famine and made our way back to the Fort.

Summer came. The agent gave out a few potatoes to the Indians to plant. Some actually did plant them; others were so hungry that they ate what was given them. Also, in the early spring they scraped the inner bark of pine and cottonwood, and dug "pomme blanche," a tuberous growth something like a turnip, for food. Then came fishing time, and they caught trout. Somehow they got through the summer, and then came winter again, the starvation winter—the winter of death, as it was called—and from which ever afterward everything was dated.

In his annual report, the agent had written at great length

about the heathenish rites of his people, but had said little of their needs. He told of the many hundred acres they had planted with potatoes and turnips—they may have planted five acres all told. In fact, he gave no hint of the approaching calamity. For years in his annual report he had recorded a constant increase in the tribe's resources; he would not now, it seemed, take back his words and make himself out a liar. It had been through his own single, strenuous efforts that the Blackfeet had risen to their present stage of civilization, "but their heathenish rites were most deplorable."

At the agency, old Almost-a-dog, day after day, checked off the deaths of the starved ones. Women crowded around the windows of the agent's office, held up their skinny children to his gaze, and asked for a cup of flour or rice or beans or corn—anything, in fact, that would appease hunger.

He waved them away. "Go," he would say surlily. "Go away! I have nothing for you." Of course he hadn't. The $30,000 appropriated for the Blackfeet had disappeared.

The Indian ring got a part, and the rest, from which must be subtracted a freight tariff of 5 cents per pound, was used to buy many unnecessary things. Beef and flour were what the people needed, and did not get. In one part of the stockade the agent kept about fifty chickens, a couple of tame wild geese and some ducks, which were daily fed an abundance of corn, freighted all the way from Sioux City up to Fort Benton by steamboat, and then more than a hundred miles overland, for the use of the Indians. The corn was Government property, which, by law, the agent could neither buy nor in any way convert to his own use. Nevertheless, he fed it liberally to his hens, and the Indian mothers stood around mournfully watching, and furtively picking up a kernel of the grain here and there. And day by day the people died. There were several thousand pounds of this grain, but the chickens needed it.

The news of all this did not reach us until February, when Wolf Head came in one day riding the sorriest horse I ever saw. It had a little hair in places, the skin along the back was wrinkled, and here and there had been deeply frozen. "There

are not many of them up there that look better," said Wolf
Head, sadly. "Most of our herds are dead." And then he went
on to tell of the starving and dying people. Nät-ah'-ki and the
Crow Woman were quickly heating some food and coffee, which
they placed on the table before Wolf Head. Never in my life
did I see food disappear so quickly, in such huge portions. I
arose after a little and took the different things away. "You
shall have them later," I said. The woman protested until I
convinced them that starving people sometimes die when given
much food after their long fast. In the evening our place was
well filled with the Indians from camp, and Wolf Head repeated
what he had told us.

When Wolf Head ended his tale, the men sat very still, not
even smoking, and then they began, one by one, to heap such
curses on their agent and white men in general as their language permitted. Berry and I listened in silence; we knew they
did not mean us—we knew that they regarded us as members
of their tribe, their own people. But we were nevertheless
ashamed before them, sore that the cupidity and carelessness
and lust for land of the white race had brought them and theirs
to this pass. After talk had drifted into half silences, Berry said
what he could in the way of condolence, adding, "We told you
months ago to kill that agent of yours. Had you done that, there
would have been a great excitement where the white people
live, and men would have been sent here to look into the matter.
They would have learned that you were without food, and a
plenty would have been sent to you."

I said nothing. A thought had suddenly struck me which I
at once put into execution. I sat down and wrote a letter to a
New York man with whom I had had some correspondence, but
had never met, explaining fully the sad plight the Blackfeet
were in. My story in due time reached a sympathetic hand, and
I was told to go on up to the agency and write an account of
what I saw there. Unknown to me this gentleman had ridden
several trails in the West and had formed a different opinion
of Indians from what most white men have.

The Indian police had been ordered by the agent to arrest

every white man they found on the reservation. If I rode right
into the stockade, the police would have to arrest me or resign,
and I wished none of them to leave the service, for the agent
gave them plenty of food for themselves and families. Therefore, I rode from one camp to another for a day, and what I saw
was a heart-rending repetition of my previous visit with the
Piegans.

Leaving the vicinity of the agency, I rode over to Birch Creek,
the southern boundary of the reservation, where there was a
small camp. A few range cattle were wintering in the vicinity,
and the hunters occasionally went out in the night and killed
one, thoroughly covering up or removing all traces of the kill.
The cattlemen knew of course that their herds were growing
smaller, but they could prove nothing, so they merely damned
the Indians and talked about "wiping them off the face of the
earth." Even that last remnant of the Blackfeet's once vast
territory, their reservation, was coveted by the great cattle
kings.

CHAPTER 29

The Black Robe's Help

DURING my visits to the various camps, I had heard much of a certain Black Robe whom the people called Stahk'-tsi kye-wak-sin—Eats-in-the-middle-of-the-day. "He is a man," the people told me. "Twice the agent has ordered him off of the reservation, but he returns to talk with us, and help us as he can."

I learned that he had built a Nät-o-wap'-o yis, or sacred house, on the non-reservation side of Birch Creek, and I went there after visiting the last of the camps. I found the Rev. P. P. Prando, S. J., at home in his rude shed-like room, attached to the little log chapel, and there we two struck up a fine friendship, which was never broken.

Father Prando made me know that I was welcome, and I stopped with him for the night. We had supper; some biscuits, rancid bacon, some vile tea, no sugar. "It is all I have," he said deprecatingly. "I have given a little here, and a little there, and this is all that remains."

We began to talk about the Indians, and I learned with surprise and pleasure that Father Prando had written to Washington, without result. Then he had corresponded with the army officers at Fort Shaw, especially with General Edward A. Maule, and they had accomplished something. Reporting to the War Department the condition of the Blackfeet, there had been a lively scene between the officials of that and the Indian Department, with the result that an inspector was to be sent out. He was supposed even then to be on his way. "And now," the priest concluded, "it all depends upon the inspector. If he is honest, all will be well; if dishonest, then—" He could say no more.

Down at the trader's store I got the details of the visit of the inspector. Arrived at the stockade, he had the driver stop just within the gates. "Where is that chicken house?" he yelled, jumping from the wagon and staring at the gaunt Indians standing apathetically around. The driver pointed it out to him, and he ran and kicked open the door, shoved the chickens out and piled out after them several sacks of corn. "Here, you," he called to the astonished spectators, "take these; take the chickens and go and eat something."

If the Indians did not understand the words, they at least understood his actions—and there was a scramble for grain and fleeing, squawking hens. The inspector hurried on across to the office, kicked open the door and came face to face with the agent, who had arisen, and was staring at him in astonishment. "You God-damned canting old hypocrite," he cried. "I've just given your Indians those chickens, and some Government corn. What do you mean by denying that your charges are starving?"

"They are not starving," the agent replied. "I will admit that they haven't a large ration, but they are not starving by any means. But what right have you, breaking in here and questioning me?"

"Here is my card," the inspector replied, "and I'll add that I suspend you right now. Your goose is cooked."

The agent read the card and sank back into his chair, speechless.

The inspector drew on the Fort Shaw commissary for what supplies could be spared, and bought more at Helena, but they were a long time in coming. Owing to the melting spring snow, the roads were almost impassable, so, still for a few weeks, Almost-a-dog kept cutting notches in his willow mortuary record, and at the end, after a bountiful supply of food had arrived and a new and honest agent was looking out for their welfare, the total numbered five hundred and fifty-five! Nearly one-fourth of the tribe had died. The living, weakened by their long privation, became an easy prey to tuberculosis in its various forms.

I had to go back to tell the good priest that his efforts had proved more than successful, and thus I stayed another night with him. He told me of his work with the Crows, among whom he had been for several years, long enough, in fact, to learn their language. Like most of those frontier Jesuits, he could do many things: he had a good knowledge of medicine and surgery; he could build a log cabin; repair a broken wagon wheel; survey and construct an irrigating ditch; and he was a successful fisherman and good shot.

I came across him one afternoon far down on Milk River. He had been visiting some distant parishioners, and had tethered out his horses for a short rest. He was broiling something over a small fire, and looking up, invited me to alight and eat with him. "It is a badger," he said, "that I have just killed."

"But," I expostulated, "they are not good to eat. I never heard of anyone eating badgers, did you?"

"My son," he replied, deliberately turning the meat over the glowing coals, "everything that God has made has some use, if we could only discern it. This badger now, He made it; I am very hungry; therefore, I broil its meat—I killed it and it is mine—and I shall satisfy my hunger."

"But see here!" I went on, dismounting and sitting down by his fire, "when you are traveling around this way, why don't you have a grub box in your wagon?"

"I had; there is the box, you see; but save for a little salt and pepper, it is now empty. The people I visited were very poor, and I gave them all I had."

The very last of the buffalo herds disappeared in 1883. In

the spring of 1884 a large flotilla of steamboats was tied up at
the Fort Benton levee; among them the "Black Hills" and
"Dacotah," boats of great size and carrying capacity. The latter
came up but once in a season—when the Missouri was bank-
full from the melting snow in the mountains—and this was
their last trip for all time to come. The railroad was coming.
It had already crossed Dakota, and was creeping rapidly across
the Montana plains.

When the railroad did finally enter the Rocky Mountain
country, a branch running to Fort Benton, Great Falls, Helena,
and Butte, the main line crossing the divide through the Two
Medicine Pass, it brought in its coaches many immigrants from
the States, at whom the oldtimers laughed. "What are they
coming here for?" they asked. "What are they going to do—
these hard-hatted men and delicate-looking women?"

They soon found out. The newcomers settled here and there
in the valleys, and took up the available water rights; they
opened stores in the towns and crossroads places and reduced
prices to a five-cent basis; they even gave exact change in
pennies. Heretofore a spool of thread, even a lamp-wick, had
been sold for two bits. The old storekeepers and traders, with
their easy, liberal ways, could not hold their own in this new
order of things; they could not change their life-long habits,
and one by one they went to the wall.

The men married to Indian women—squawmen, as they
were contemptuously called—suffered most, and, strange to
say, the wives of the newcomers, not the men, were their bit-
terest enemies. They forbade their children to associate with
the half-breed children, and at school the position of the latter
was unbearable. The white ones beat them and called them
opprobrious names. This hatred of the squawman was even
carried into politics.

One of them, as clean-minded, genial, fearless, and honest
a man as I ever knew, was nominated for sheriff of the county
upon the party ticket which always carried the day; but at that
election he alone of all the candidates of his party was not
elected. He was actually snowed under. The white women had

so badgered their husbands and brothers, had so vehemently protested against the election of a squawman to any office, that they succeeded in accomplishing his defeat. And so, one by one, these men moved to the only place where they could live in peace, where there was not an enemy within a hundred and more miles of them, the reservation; and there they settled to pass their remaining days. There were forty-two of them at one time; few are left.

Let me correct the general impression of the squawmen, at least as to those I have known, the men who married Blackfeet women. In the days of the Indians' dire extremity, they gave them all they could, and were content so long as there remained a little bacon and flour for their families; and some days there was not even that in the houses of some of them, for they had given their all. With the Indian they starved for a time, perchance. Scattered here and there upon the reservation, they built for themselves neat homes and corrals, and fenced their hay lands, all of which was an object lesson to the Indian.

But they did more than that. They helped to build their red neighbors' cabins and stables; surveyed their irrigating ditches; taught them how to plough and to manage a mowing machine—all this without thought of pay or profit. If you enter the home of a Blackfoot, you nearly always find the floor clean, the windows spotless, everything about in perfect order, the sewing machine and table covered with pretty cloths; the bed with clean, bright-hued blankets; the cooking utensils and tableware spotless and bright. No Government field-matrons have taught them to do this, for they have had none. This they learned by observing the ways of the squawmen's wives. I have seen hundreds of white homes—there are numbers of them in any city—so exceedingly dirty, their inmates so slovenly, that one turns from them in absolute disgust; but I have seen nothing like that among the Blackfeet.

In their opulent days—under a good agent, and when they had numbers of steers to sell—they bought much furniture, even good carpets. There came to me one day at that time a friend, and we smoked together. "You have a book with pictures of furniture," he said. "Show me the best bedstead it tells about."

I complied. "There it is," pointing to the cut. "All brass, best of springs; price eighty dollars."

"Send for it," he said, "I want it. It costs only two steers, and what is that?"

"There are others," I went on, "just as good-looking, part iron, part brass, which cost much less."

"Huh!" he exclaimed. "Old Tail-feathers-coming-over-the-hill has one that cost fifty dollars. I'm going to have the best."

Without the squawman, I do not know what the Blackfeet would have done in the making of their treaties with the Government; in getting rid of agents, of whom the less said the better—for the squawman fought their battles and bore the brunt of all the trouble. I have known an agent to order his police to kill a certain squawman on sight, because the man had reported his thievery to Washington; and others to order squawmen to leave the reservation, separating them from their families because they had spoken too openly regarding certain underhand doings. But at intervals there were good, honest, capable men in charge, under whom the Indians regained in a measure the prosperity they had lost. But such men did not last; with a change of administration they were always dismissed by the new powers.

One thing the squawmen never succeeded in doing—they were never able to rid the reservation of the great cattle kings' stock. The big men had an understanding with some agents, and at other times with certain politicians of great influence. So their stock remained and increased and fed down the rich grasses. Most of the Indians and most of the squawmen carefully tended their little herds in some favorable locality as near as possible to their homes; but always, once in the spring, once in the fall, the great roundup of the cattle kings swept like wildfire across the reservation. Thirty or forty swift riders would swoop down on one of these little herds. Some of their cattle would be mixed in with them; but they did not stop to cut them out; there wasn't time; and they drove them all to some distant point or branding corral, and the owner of the little herd lost forever more or less of them.

At last, so I am told, the Indians prevailed upon the Department to fence the south and east sides of the reservation in order to keep the foreign stock out, and their own inside. There was no need of fencing the west and north sides, for the Rocky Mountains form the western boundary, and the Canadian line the northern. It cost $30,000 to build that fence, and then the cattle kings obtained permission to pasture 30,000 head of cattle within it. But perhaps it is as well. It is only hastening the end a bit, for the Blackfeet, as I have said before, are to have their lands allotted. Then will come the sheepmen, desolation in their wake, and then the end.

The Department has decreed that no able-bodied person should receive rations. In that bleak country there is no chance of obtaining work, for the white men's ranches are few and far between. Even if a man obtained three months' work in summer—something almost impossible—his wages could not by any means support his family for a year. A friend wrote me in January: "I was over on the reservation today and visited many old friends. In most of the homes there was little, generally no food, and the people were sitting sadly around the stove, drinking wild tea."

In the hegira of the oldtimers to the reservation, Berry and I took part. Fort Conrad had been sold. Berry bought out the reservation trader, goodwill and goods, for three hundred dollars.

I got an insane idea in my head that I wanted to be a sheepman, and locating some fine springs and hay ground about twelve miles above Fort Conrad, I built some good sheds, and a house, and put up great stacks of hay. The cattlemen burned me out. I guess they did right, for I had located the only water for miles around. I left the blackened ruins and followed Berry. I am glad that they did burn me out, for I thus can truthfully say that I had no part in the devastation of Montana's once lovely plains.

We built us a home, Nät-ah'-ki and I, in a lovely valley

where the grass grew green and tall. We were a long time building it. Up in the mountains where I cut the logs, our camp under the towering pines was so pleasant that we could hardly leave it for a couple of days to haul home a wagonload of material. And there were so many pleasant diversions that the axe leaned up against a stump during long dreamy days, while we went trout fishing, or trailed a deer or bear, or just remained in camp listening to the wind in the pine tops, watching the squirrels steal the remains of our breakfast, or an occasional grouse strutting by. But before snow came, we had our house built and furnished and were content.

We had a growing bunch of cattle which were rounded up with the other reservation stock twice a year. I built two small irrigating ditches and raised some hay. There was little work to do, and we made a trip somewhere every autumn, up in the Rockies with friends, or took a skiff and idly drifted and camped along the Missouri for three or four hundred miles below Fort Benton, then home by rail.

We were always glad to return home. "How peaceful it all is here," Nät-ah'-ki used to say.

The years passed happily for Nät-ah'-ki and me. But neither of us could ever forget another kind of happiness our life once held—the thrill of the free, open plains, of seeing a shaggy brown sea of buffalo as far as the eye could reach, or the sharp evenings when I rode home after a good hunt to my comfortable lodge of skins, its cheerful fire, and the warm kindness of our Piegan friends and kinsfolks.

THE END